NORTH STAR PLATOON

AND A GUARDIAN ANGEL

DARRELL HAMLIN

ISBN: 1470050749
ISBN 13: 9781470050740

From the author

Through the years, I have often discussed with my students the issue of "fate." We have had lengthy conversations as to why things happen and have tried to figure out if there is an explanation for why evil events take place. It is hard to justify to children who have been victimized by family, friends, and the system that there is a God with an actual plan to help them through their journey.

For me, teaching at Region 5 Learning Center was not an act of fate or destiny; it was an answer to a prayer.

In 1982, I was unemployed, single, and bored. Traveling south bound in my 1976 MGB sports car on North Pearl Street in Tacoma, Washington, I was headed toward Point Defiance Park for a five-mile run on the trails.

At North 11th and Pearl Street, halted at a red stoplight, my destiny was about to change.

For no conscience reason, I changed my future and made a right turn toward my house. Three blocks later, I noticed a track meet at Wilson High School, the school I myself had graduated from.

Like iron to a magnet, I was drawn to the event.

Noticing that the finish line of the 3200 meter run was disorganized, a little voice inside of me said, "Help out." Without being asked, I stepped in to sort out the finishers. As I was leaving, my former track coach Sam Ring approached and asked if I wanted to be his assistant coach. Of course, I jumped at the opportunity.

While coaching over the next three years, I earned my teacher's degree from Central Washington University in History and Political Science.

I did not plan on being a teacher. A right-hand turn, at a red light changed my course in life. Was it fate, karma, luck or a Guardian Angel guiding my path? I believe it was my Guardian Angel.

From that point forward, several incidents occurred guiding me toward my eventual teaching position at Region 5 Learning Center working with students on parole and probation. Protected by my Guardian Angel, I've worked with juveniles on parole or probation for the last twenty-four years without injury.

Region 5 Learning Center and the outdoor adventures that the parole or probation students and I have taken changed our lives.

Darrell Hamlin

A note to the reader; to protect the identity
of individuals mentioned in this book,
I have changed all of the names
within my non-fiction narrative
as well as within excerpts
from publications and
correspondence.

Thank you.

To the student adventurers of the
Region 5 Learning Center,
may you be living in peace.

CONTENTS

MOUNT RAINIER NATIONAL PARK

1. Big D

─────────

It happened in what seemed like slow motion. Without reacting, watching my air compressor descend out of control to the ground from the back of my SUV, I asked myself, "Why Lord do things like this have to happen?"

"Is there a reason why?"

Hearing air whoosh from my compressor's now broken air regulator valve, my goal for a solid uninterrupted day's work on our family Ohop Lake cabin was now in jeopardy.

After unloading the rest of the tools and locking them in the cabin, I wended my way along the oil soaked gravel road towards town. Fifteen minutes away, Eatonville, which wasn't much more than two streets and the bare necessities, was my only hope for compressor parts.

Being about a forty-five minute drive from Tacoma, Washington where I live, rural Eatonville was small and undeveloped. Surrounded by evergreen fir trees, it was tucked peacefully into the Cascade Mountain foothills like a shiny Christmas ornament snuggled within. It's a post-logging community where you do not see many minorities. Unfortunately, like many small towns in the Pacific Northwest, during the 1990's "methamphetamines" had become the evil addicting drug of choice.

Driving down one of the only two main streets, I noticed a very large African-American man wearing a dirty well worn Mexican poncho. Catching my attention, he was easily pushing two old rusting shopping carts. Impressive to see was his coordinated efforts in manipulating both carts in a forward motion down the narrow sidewalk.

Odd in appearance, the Mexican poncho looked like a huge multi-colored blanket draped over a moving object while balanced by a head protruding through it. The slit seemed barely open enough for his large head to squeeze through. In Eatonville, his homeless appearance didn't fit into the small-town landscape.

Curious, watching in amazement, with one of the front black rubber wheels trying to wiggling free, he easily pushed both carts from a sideways position perfecting the strategy. Missing the plastic store logoed handles, the shopping carts had blankets and other street survival tools neatly stashed inside the cage on wheels. The only thing missing from his modern day "Rockwell" hobo appearance was a small ragged dog tagging along flapping its tongue while inside one of the carts.

Turning left at the yellow blinking light toward the only hardware store, it dawned on me that this large man resembled a former student of mine. Nicknamed "Big D," Dirk Witfield was a student that I'd befriended while teaching as a Para-educator at Mason Junior High School in Tacoma, Washington.

Strange how memories emerge—flashing back, I could recall Big D vividly. It had been years since I'd seen him, and trying to figure out the clues, he had married a young lady from Eatonville. So it could be him. Why else would a huge African American be wondering the streets of Eatonville?

Instantly, a visual of running into Big D's large mass on the Hilltop area of Tacoma flashed in. Wearing a huge pride-filled smile, he proudly showed me his children's 3x4 inch standard school pictures held in his battered brown leather wallet by faded plastic sleeves.

With bits of images flashing through like pieces of faded memory highlights, I thought, "After all these years, could this guy actually be Big D?"

After purchasing the needed, but not exact compressor parts, not seeing Big D where I projected him to be, I began searching for him by meandering through the unpaved side streets of Eatonville. Canvassing the area, I reflected on how it was a weird coincidence how I'd ended up at Mason Junior High School in the first place.

At the time, I was roofing houses and coaching track and field at Wilson High School. One evening, while grocery shopping, I bumped into a previous girlfriend in the fruits and vegetables section. All smiles, she shared, told me with great enthusiasm about a special education Para-educator position at Mason Junior High that she was sadly giving up.

"You will just love it!" was her long and lasting comment.

Soon to be leaving town, she neglected to tell me how disturbed and mean the students in this program were. Given the difficulty of the position, I have often wondered if she was trying to get back at me for breaking up with her.

Big D was placed in the program as a severely behavioral disorder student or "SBD." He was a very angry young man and supposedly he could not mentally control his behavior.

Once hired, I was the naïve twenty-two-year-old teacher's aide all fired up and ready to make a difference. Raised in a somewhat "normal" Christian family, I was caught totally off guard by the unpredictable malicious behaviors of the students.

Bid D was the worst of the bunch.

At first, I found it odd that Big D did not talk very much. He was a huge guy who felt at ease just observing situations unfold around him. I also learned quickly that he had a dark side, almost possessed by the devil at times. When he lost it, everyone cleared out of his way; yet, at other times, he was as gentle as a teddy bear.

Reflecting back, it was as if he was having a tug of war between good and evil. He was a weird mix—some days he was throwing desks, screaming, and cussing. Other days, he was gentle and kind. He could read well, had a great memory, and could recall historical events easily. But, the dark side of Big D was scary, and I am sure that his immense size and appearance made a lot of people nervous.

I admit, I felt sorry for Big D, he seemed angry, sad, and alone. As large as he was, other students were intimidated and stayed away from him. While working with him, I often wondered, "What evil event could have turned him into such an angry guy?"

I never asked and he never talked about it.

At the time, I had no idea how to handle his anger other than to just spend positive time with him. My inner voice, my Guardian Angel was leading the way.

Acquiring permission from the teacher, Debra Feller, I started to build a relationship with Big D during school hours. To break the barriers between us, after lunch, without drawing suspicion, I would follow Big D to the gym and urge him out to play basketball.

In regard to Debra Fellers, she was an excellent role model in dealing with out of their minds kids. She reminded me of the testimonials written of calm reacting sergeants under intense fire during the World War II Omaha Beach landing giving life saving commands. With daily swearing and mean behaviors bulleting all around us, she would calmly fire out commands expecting conformity.

In regard to my future challenges as a learning specialist with students who were on parole and probation, Debra taught me more about calmly defusing dangerous situations that any other teacher, professor or class ever did. She was amazing.

As time and activities passed, Big D and I developed a positive friendship. He seemed to be responding favorably to our developing relationship, so I asked the counselor for her advice regarding spending more time with him outside of the school day.

Being very curt, she blurted out, "If you spend time with him, it's for life!"

At the time that she'd hastily blurted it out, I thought she was serious, "For life?"

Later, I learned that students like Big D come and go. If she had thought before she spoke, she would have said, "If you spend time with these students, their memories will stay with you for life." That better sums up the experiences of working with street kids.

As it turned out, under that volcanic anger, Big D had a lot more kindness and common sense than most people upon first impression would expect. He was a large intimidating figure of a man, but he could be very polite and thankful too.

Oddly, spending more time with Big D, he still did not talk very much.

Building trust outside the confines of the school setting was tough. Big D and I started off going to high school sporting events. On several occasions, while driving to an outing or fishing off the dock of our Ohop Lake cabin, we would just sit in silence. Coming from an outspoken family, it took time for me to adjust to the quietness. I was always trying to come up with conversations, but, after awhile, I gave up and learned to enjoy the peace and quiet.

As memory after memory flashed through my thoughts, I continued to drive around Eatonville searching for Big D. Driving the side streets, past the skate park and lastly to the Riverside Park just outside of town finding no trace. With my window half down, as the river raged by, I was thinking to myself, "Where could he have gone to in such a small town?"

Puzzled, I knew that Eatonville was too small to escape unnoticed.

Turning around and exiting the Riverside Park, another situation that I recall with Big D emerged like a ray of light on a cloudy day.

After a drunk, stoned punk teenage driver ran a stop sign and I t-boned his car, Big D unknowingly made me some money. Not being at fault in the accident, I was having negotiation problems with the insurance claims adjuster. He was trying to intimidate me into settling for less money than I wanted. Hiding behind the receiver, he was loud, rude, and abrasive on the phone. Wanting to state my case face to face, I decided to talk to the bully-man claims adjuster in person.

Swinging through the Hilltop area of Tacoma, I recall picking up Big D for an outing on my way to the insurance adjuster's office.

In the early 1980s, the Hilltop area where Big D lived had its crime, but it was not yet dominated by 23rd Street Hilltop Crips gang and their destructive activities.

Tacoma has the twelfth deepest international commercial seaport in the world and is a working-class community. The Hilltop area is located about a mile above the city center and international shipping facilities and was a rough low-income area.

Reflecting back, I have to smile. It must have been a humorous sight to see us riding in the same car. Being five foot ten inches tall and probably weighing 155 pounds, Big D was six foot five and weighed 250 pounds or more. By the time he was packed into my 1976 Toyota GT coupe, his massive body spilled over to my side and out his open window. Riding with him was quite cozy.

Once in the insurance building, we were directed to the adjuster's small windowless office. After introductions, Big D, a man of few words, grabbed a seat and sat quietly.

Once seated, anxious, I started my rehearsed speech that I'd practiced in front of the mirror: "Listen, I should get the exact amount in damages that I have requested. I was not at fault and…"

About halfway through my concerns, during which the bully-man had been acting fidgety and uncomfortable, he raised his hands to cut me off. Pausing like a black and white striped referee in a flagrant hacking foul situation, he eked out, "There must have been a misunderstanding."

Glancing slightly at Big D, he nervously dribbled out, "I, I, I made an error. You will receive the total amount of damages you requested."

After giving the bully-man a "what the heck look," glancing over at Big D, I shook my head, and said, "Let's go."

It was not until years later, after running into Big D on the Hilltop that I figured out why bully-man had settled with me so quickly. Big D must have made an intimidating impression without saying a single word.

Continuing the search for Big D, I was almost ready to give up when a little voice whispered upon me to pull into the only grocery store in town. Once maneuvered into an isolated parking slot, talking aloud, I asked, "How could he disappear in Eatonville?"

"Where could he have gone?"

Frustrated, I kept thinking, "As out of place as he was, he has to be here somewhere."

My aim was simple, I just wanted to tell him what a blessing it was that he was still alive.

Glancing around in despair, I spotted Big D's carts stranded next to a corner flagpole. Slipping out of my SUV, I moved quickly.

Glancing from side to side, crossing the street, I approaching the abandoned shopping carts like a thief in the night. Like the snapping of a damp towel against the bare rump of an unsuspecting victim in the gym locker room, the flapping of the American flag fighting in the wind became noticeably louder and louder.

Looking around and not seeing Big D, I concluded that the only logical place for him to have gone was into the small diner kitty-corner to the flagpole. It was a dull pink eatery that I hadn't noticed before.

Gaining nervous confidence, entering the diner, casually I noticed several mismatched small antique pink plastic-covered tables and multi-colored chairs scattered aimlessly about.

Attracting my attention, a cheaply brush-painted blackboard food menu stood out on the light pink wall like a black eye. On the left side of the menu, the white-chalked prices had been recklessly smeared and haphazardly scribbled back on.

The shadowed numbers reminded me of an old slate chalkboard from an abandoned one-room schoolhouse. The smeared images left a ghostly white residue of previous attempts to find an acceptable price for meals.

Cautiously looking around, a heavy-set man with a dirty apron was posted up in front of what appeared to be the kitchen, dining bar and cash register. His body language was almost begging for an order, any order.

Out of the corner of my eye, without an obvious look, I tried to get an unsuspecting glance at Big D.

Pausing, I silently recall wondering, "So many years, would he even remember me? What would he remember, the movies, fishing trips, digging a well at the Lake Cabin or just spending quiet time together?"

Admittedly, standing there sneaking a look at Big D, I was questioning my motivations. It felt as if I were going before a judge for a grand jury indictment.

Approaching, without an obvious look, I noticed Big D was slowly sipping what appeared to be vegetable soup, the type with alphabet letters aimlessly floating around.

Quietly savoring every meticulous slurp, Big D reminded me of a soup commercial on TV of a little kid coming in from a cold snowy winter day to warm himself up before venturing back out again to play.

Odd, next to Big D's soup bowl were two tall stacks of plastic packaged saltine crackers. The glossy packaged crackers with serrated edges were perfectly aligned. They reminded me of the former New York Twin Towers before the horrible unprovoked 9-11-01 attack by terrorists.

Pausing again, before uttering a word, I noticed that his cloth napkin was neatly placed on his large stomach with one corner perfectly tucked into his smudged t-shirt. His well worn Mexican poncho was posted upright across from him as if it were a friend waiting for its own bowl of soup.

Slowly turning to partially face Big D, I conveyed, "You look familiar to me. Have we met?"

Locking eyes, I felt my forehead crunch together with the feeling of concern. As time slowed, I was not sure if I recognized his frightened expression or not.

"Is that you, D?" I cautiously asked.

Looking in silence, I could see by the expression on his face, that he was startled. Glancing up with eyes only, without breaking eye contact, he slowly shook his head from side to side.

As time began to regain its normal pace, maintaining eye contact, in a timid whisper he said, "I don't know you."

Looking into his deep bloodshot brown eyes, I didn't know if I knew him either. But, I have seen those eyes a thousand times before. His eyes expressed the story of a person who felt despair, tattered, hurt, and worn out. Knowing the look, slightly backing off to give him more space, I explained gently, "You remind me of an old friend."

"I am sorry to have bothered you."

With his soup spoon suspended in mid-air, he did not speak again.

Trying to break eye contact, I noticed that his spoon slightly trembled. Almost in slow motion tiny droplets of soup, without the alphabet letters, slowly dribbled onto the faded pink plastic tablecloth, *plop, plop, plop.*

For some odd reason, I watched as the escaping droplets were slightly missing the Twin Towers stack of saltine crackers before splattering on the table.

Finally breaking eye contact, I slowly moved away.

My exit from the small diner was quick and quiet. Not looking both ways for cars, rambling across the street, I unconsciously scrambled into my vehicle. My thoughts for safety were elsewhere.

After time regained its normal pace, safely in the protection of my vehicle, I noticed that it was raining.

Glancing toward the carts through the droplets of rain on the side window, I wondered, "How did this large homeless African-American man end up in the small town of Eatonville?"

Blankly watching his neatly stacked possessions getting rained upon, noticing the American flag fighting off the rain as it wavered in the wind, I sadly pondered, "where will this man end up?"

"Lord, where did Big D end up?"

2. The Box

R unning into who I thought was Big D triggered a sad memory that occurred during my first contracted teaching position with Tacoma Public Schools.

Several years after meeting Big D, earning my teacher's degree, I stumbled into a teaching position at a small alternative learning center for juveniles that were on parole or probation. Region 5 Learning Center was a joint venture between Tacoma Public Schools and the Washington State Juvenile Rehabilitation Administration, JRA. JRA was divided into ten different regions across the state. Pierce County, Washington, was Region 5.

Being on parole or probation, our court-appointed students were between the ages of fifteen to seventeen. Generally we did not get eighteen-year-olds—they were usually sent to the adult Pierce County jail or prison.

During my first few years at Region 5 Learning Center, still in contact with Dirk, Big D, I felt no obligation professionally to do so. I just liked hanging around him. He was thankful for the time we spent together and was very courteous. Being single, I had extra time on my hands.

Sadly, Big D had been arrested and convicted of assault and sent to the Maple Lane juvenile prison. Not asking him about his crime, I thought that if he wanted me to know about it, he would have told me. I tried to make it a point to visit him once or twice a month. Leaving Tacoma at two in the afternoon, traveling south on Interstate 5, I could be at Maple Lane within an hour.

Reflecting back, it is a shame that Dirk did not go into the armed services. He was an intelligent guy who needed structure and discipline.

During one visit with Dirk, I learned a valuable lesson regarding institutional safety. He did not talk very much, so when he did, it was a matter of importance. On this occasion, Big D calmly informed me, "It is dangerous to wear a necktie when working with criminals."

Pausing to get the right words, he went on, "A guard got jumped here and was strangled from behind by his own necktie."

Being naïve to the criminal mind, I was very appreciative of Dirk's warning. Taking him seriously, from that day forward and to this day, I only wear clip-on ties to work. It gave me a comforting feeling that he was concerned about my safety.

While visiting Dirk at the institution, we would play checkers, chess, or just sit in silence. Thanks to my Grandpa Packard, I could give him a run for his money in checkers. In regard to chess, being luckier than most, my father taught me how to play a tactical game. But when challenging Big D in chess, all that training did not help with the weekly butt kicking's I received. Never able to beat him, he was calculating and always several steps ahead of my every move.

On several occasions the guards informed me that I was Dirk's only visitor. It was sad to think that I was the only outside support that he had. Knowing that I worked at Region 5 Learning Center helped—the guards gave me the feeling of having an inside connection. They would keep me apprised of Dirk's progress.

One day, getting ready to leave the Region 5 building, Leona, our secretary at the time informed me that I had a phone call from Maple Lane. Leona knew about Big D and the importance.

Caught off guard, I thought, "Dirk does not have the money to call long distance." I was suspicious, "Who would want to talk to me from the Lane?"

In a serious, stern voice, an unidentified Maple Lane staff informed me, "Dirk is in twenty-three/one solitary confinement." Meaning, he is only out of his cell for one hour a day. I recognized the guard's voice, but not his name. "He's having a rough time and tearing the place up."

Asking the guard why, he simply replied, "Dirk is going off. Can you pay him a visit?"

Dirk was a very large and strong young man; I am sure that it took several guards to contain him and force him into solitary confinement.

After school the following day, anxiously, I hustled southbound on Interstate 5 to see Dirk. Showing my identification, security waved me in as usual. I always got a weird feeling driving through the prison security gates at the Lane. It has always been odd to me that we have to lock people up for the protection of others.

Entering the administrative building and introducing myself, I was escorted outside to a small cinderblock complex that I had never noticed before. The square dull gray windowless building was hidden at the far corner of the electric fence-enclosed Maple Lane prison.

Entering and adjusting to the smell of sweat and urine, I was directed to Dirk's tiny cell. Peering through a small smudged window, I witnessed an unrecognizable Big D. His eyes were puffy, his hair was a mess, and his orange prison jumpsuit was ripped in several places. The presents of evil surrounded me.

Peering in at Big D, I had no idea what could have sent him into such a rage. Banging on the medal door to get his attention, we made eye contact through the small rectangular wired window. I could tell by his bloodshot eyes that he had been crying for some time.

Barely glancing up from the floor, with his head angled he hollered, "Go away!"

"D!" I yelled through the thick metal door. "It's me! Darrell!"

Raising his head and hollering like a man, he yelled back, "They wouldn't even let me say good bye!"

"D, talk to me!" I yelled again, "What's going on?"

"He's dead, I didn't even get to see him off," he said in a whimper.

Letting the moment hang, I tried to figure out whom he was talking about. I knew that his older brother Dwight was attending Lincoln High School, and from what I understood, he was doing well in school. His little brother had never been in trouble from what I recalled. It was not his mother, Harriet, because Dirk had said "he."

Trying to regroup my thoughts, I asked, "D, you have to tell me what's going on for me to understand."

"He is dead and they didn't let me go to the funeral," he said in a tired, worn-out voice.

"Who is dead?"

Letting several slow motion seconds pass, I had no idea what to say. Meeting Dirk's family, I remembered him telling me that his older brother Dwight was a Blood gang member. At the time Dirk told me, I thought that it was dangerous to be an Eastside Blood in the heart of the Hilltop Crips gang territory. Dirk and his family actually lived near the main base of the 23rd Street Hilltop Crips. "Was it him?" I thought, struggling to think clearly.

Trying to piece together the events that must have taken place, Dirk screamed, "Go, away!" Taking a long final heartfelt look, respecting his wishes, I did not press the issue further and left.

As we were leaving the dreary solitary confinement building, I was still shocked at seeing Dirk in such a state of mind. Breaking into my disillusionment, the security guard who'd escorted me to the area quietly informed me, "Dirk made something for you."

Lost in thought with what I had just witnessed, passively I followed the guard.

Not making eye contact, the guard said, "I am not sure if I should give it to you or not, but I saw your name on the bottom of it."

Pausing, he said, "I thought that Dirk would want you to have it."

Once we were back in the normalcy of the administrative building, the guard went behind the security counter and respectfully handed me a beautifully crafted white oak wood box. The box was a vertical rectangular shape with a lid. Analyzing the box, I could not help but dwell on how mournful Dirk had looked in solitary confinement. Amazed at the perfectly made wooden box, I could not visualize the two events of good and evil simultaneously.

"When did he make this?" I asked without looking up.

"Dirk has been taking wood shop classes and seems to enjoy it."

Holding the box with both hands like a fragile carton of eggs, looking at the security guard I commented, "This is perfect."

The security guard paused and then said, "Dirk is a perfectionist."

Taking a closer look at the box, I noticed that the clasp and screws were perfectly placed on the front center of the box and latched with ease. The hinges that held the lid were perfectly placed one-third distance apart on the back edge of the box. The lid closed smoothly without making a sound. Turning the box upside down, I read the clearly printed message on the bottom: To my friend Darrell, from Dirk.

I recall getting a goose-bumps feeling holding back the tears that I felt coming. Not saying it to the guard, I was wondering, "How could a guy with so much anger create something as beautiful as this?"

I still have the box in my possession to this day.

Snapping me out of my amazement, the guard sympathetically said, "Dirk's brother was killed."

Stunned, I asked, "Which brother died?"

The guard simply responded, "Another gang killing."

Murder case against 2 gang members goes to jury

CHARGES GROW OUT OF 2 SLAYINGS NEAR LINCOLN HIGH SCHOOL

BY SUSAN GORDON   **DECEMBER 1991**

The News Tribune

A Pierce County Superior Court jury is to begin deliberating this morning in the trial of two Hilltop Crips gang members accused as accomplices in the July slayings of two Blood gang rivals in a shootout near Lincoln High School.

The men are accused of first-degree murder in the July 27 killings of Dwight Witfield, 21, and Albert Anderson, 24.

The two men were shot to death when Crips and Bloods clashed outside an after-hours club at 3611 S. G St. The victims got into an argument with about 15 or 20 Crips standing outside the club.

When Witfield tried to drive away, four or five gunmen opened fire on the car. Witfield was killed by a .41-caliber round that went through his car door. He died with a 9mm pistol clutched in his hand, according to prosecutors and charging papers.

Anderson was struck in the head and died the next day at St. Joseph hospital.

Dalton and McCoy, who are described by authorities as prominent members of the Hilltop Crips gang, also were charged with assault and attempted murder in connection with the incident.

These men were gunned down without any justification except that two of them were believed to be Bloods.

A witness told investigators he asked the gunmen why they were shooting at his friend; they responded by shouting obscenities and calling him a "slob" - a derogatory term for a Bloods gang member.

Then four or five gunmen opened fire at the witness and another man, although they were able to drive away unharmed.

Earlier in the trial, two other Crips gang members, Darnell Wilson, 19, and Andrew Jefferson, 18, pleaded guilty to two counts of first-degree manslaughter, prosecutors said.

Jefferson admitted firing the fatal .41-caliber bullet that killed Witfield.

After locating and reading the newspaper article, I could understand why Dirk Witfield was so upset. "I didn't get to say goodbye", still echoes in my memory.

Once Big D was out of twenty-three/one lock-up, I continued to see Dirk, but he was not the same. He had lost the positive survival spirit that drew me to him. He never talked about the murder of his older brother, Dwight, and I did not ask. How do you open up that conversation?

After Dirk's release from Maple Lane, over time, we lost contact with each other.

I have often wondered, "Where did Big D end up?"

3. Pickle Ball Champ

Not long after my experience with the man who'd I thought was Big D in Eatonville, I had an unexpected encounter with another former Region 5 Learning Center student.

The encounter occurred on a beautiful sunny Saturday in the Pacific Northwest at Peck Baseball Field in Tacoma.

Just finishing coaching my seven-year-old daughter's coach-pitch baseball game, headed for the exit, I saw a familiar face passing through the admissions gate. Not remembering his name, I knew the face. About forty yards and closing, I was confident that I knew the tall handsome man headed in my direction. It was his million-dollar smile that I recognized first.

As he walked toward me, loaded with baseball gear and my daughter in tow,

I started heading straight for him. As I walked, he tried to move out of my path. Moving directly back in front of him, he moved to his right, I moved to my left. It was a head-on collision, and there was nowhere for him to go. Looking straight into his oncoming eyes, seeing that his smile had been replaced by a look of concern, I could almost read his mind: "Who is this crazy man coming right at me?"

As we closed the gap between us, his million-dollar smile lit up like an early morning sunrise. "You shaved and cut your hair," he popped off with a huge grin.

In the traditional man-shake manner, we joined our right hands, placed them against our hearts, patted each other's right shoulder and exchanged a man hug.

Pausing, breaking the embrace, looked down at my daughter Kaylee, jokingly I said, "This is the only guy from Region 5 to have ever beaten me in full-court pickle ball."

"I beat you twice," he humorously fired back.

"It must be my age—how could I have forgotten?"

Looking down at Kaylee, he gently said, "Your dad straightened my life out."

Pausing to let the moment last, I told Kaylee, "He didn't need straightening out; he had a glowing heart and was not evil."

Still grappling to remember his name, he asked, "Do you still work at Region 5?"

"The Region 5 students were bounced out of their building for the School of the Arts students," I said and then sadly added, "Being at the bottom of the totem pole, the Tacoma School of the Arts students needed more classroom space and we were out." I went on, "The street kids in Tacoma have no voice."

Pausing as if reflecting back, he said, "I liked Region 5. I hated my probation officer, but I know now that he set me straight. Region 5 was a good school even though I wasn't supposed to be there."

"Interesting, they all say that," I chided back.

Not sure what his crime was, generally I did not ask or care. Evil had not crept into his sole like a thief in the night. He was still alive and too nice a guy to be a gangbanger. Most hard-core gangbangers by this time were either dead or in prison.

Looking into his eyes and listening to him talk about Region 5, his name popped into my thoughts like a strand of seeping sun light. Feeling relief about remembering his name, I listened as he told me, "My boy is getting into trouble, and I want to take him on a tour of Remann Hall."

"Scared straight? Isaiah," adding, "spend more time with your son, every spare second you have, spend it with him. Time is priceless." We locked eyes, and I sensed that he understood my meaning. "It is not money that makes good families," I said in a fatherly tone.

Pausing, tilting my head, I gently slipped in, "It is time spent together."

Breaking the lingering silence, I said, "Kaylee, Isaiah had a lucky day when he beat me."

"I beat you twice," he responded quickly with a laugh. "And I will beat you again."

His huge smile reflected the shared thought passing between us…if only we could.

After a man hug, we laughed and headed in opposite directions.

4. Tony's Payback

Eight years ago, the Region 5 Learning Center court-connected students were bounced out of their school on 19th and Tacoma Avenue South for the "pampered" School of the Arts students. They needed a building and having little clout, the students of Region 5 were shipped off to another location.

As a result, after fifteen years of loyal dedication, again, I was displaced from my teaching position at Region 5. It was a humiliating experience to reapply for a job that I'd had for fifteen years. It was further humiliating to be replaced by another teacher who had little if any experience working with court-connected students.

Hurt as a result of being treated so poorly, I was hoping to forget Region 5 and move on.

For the last eight years, while teaching at Pierce County's Remann Hall Juvenile Detention Center, I've compartmentalized and hidden within my subconscious the memories of Region 5 students and our adventures. Peculiar, there have recently been a series of occurrences that have led me on the journey back to the students of Region 5. I am not sure why?

Several months after running into Isaiah, an interesting incident was brought to the forefront of my consciousness. Hastily driving through the eastside of Tacoma and mentally observing nothing but my next destination, instinctively, I came to a halt at a red stoplight.

Pausing and glancing around, I recognized the area without knowing the cross streets. For some reason, my eyes were drawn to a small white house on the corner. With time at a slower pace, I recognized it to be Tony's parents' house. The paint was perfect and the lawn neatly manicured.

Lost in thought, when the red light turned to green, a honk startled me back to my speedy reality.

Back in motion, driving by the all-American modest-looking home, I began wondering, "Whatever happened to Tony?" Pondering the thought, I chuckled as the recollection of why he'd ended up at Region 5 Learning Center.

Many years before Region 5 was relocated, after one of the Life Sports road trips that we had taken to the mountains, Tony happened to be the last student to be dropped off.

Not remembering what the field trip outing was, I recalled the conversation with Tony quite clearly.

As with most occasions, the road trips would run beyond a regular school day. For liability purposes, while using the school van for transportation, I personally dropped every student off at their door step. Being cautious, I was never alone with a female student and never dropped them off last. So, alone with Tony, I had an opportunity to ask him how he'd ended up at Region 5.

Tony was not a typical Region 5 student. He was from a military family and not gang affiliated. He reminded me of a typical fun-loving young teenager. He was built like an athlete and a respectful student in class. He had not crossed into the dark side. Before our conversation, I had often wondered how such a respectful nice guy could end up at a school for court-connected students.

Pulling into his driveway, I just asked, "Tony how is it you're at Region 5?"

Tony lowered his head and said, "All I was doing was protecting my little brother."

I gave my standard teacher question, "What do you mean?"

"That guy beat up my brother for no reason!" a voice of submerged rage leaked out.

"How did you get involved?" I asked.

Tony looked directly into my eyes and said, "I caught the guy, beat him down, and took his clothes." After telling me only part of the story, in what appeared to be shame, he looked down toward the floor of the van in silence.

Not being able to figure out where the story was going, I said, "Took his what?"

Shaking his lowered head he replied, "After I beat him up, I stripped him naked in the street for messing with my brother. Then I kicked him in the butt and sent him running home."

Almost chuckling, holding it back, I drew blood from biting my lower lip. Fighting to keep the visual of a nude beat up kid running through the Eastside streets of Tacoma out of my thoughts, all I could utter out was, "Wow."

Pausing as if reliving the incident, Tony adjusted his hat, looked around, opened the van door, and before he exited calmly said, "Thanks." Without glancing back, meandering around the corner of his house, he faded out of sight.

We never talked about it again.

5. PT

C leaning out my desk one day at home, a newspaper article slipped out from a stack of messy papers. The *News Tribune* article was faded yellow from age, neatly pressed, and there was no date indicating when it had been written. Reading the article, I thought, "Why should the date matter? The story is the same, ex-gang member killed on the Hilltop."

In Tacoma during the 1980s and 1990s there were so many gang shootings, stabbings, and drive-bys that I quit reading the local newspaper. Most of the KIA, or "killed in action," during that era were current or former Region 5 students. This particular headline was different. It struck a nerve. "Man, Woman found dead in Sudan. The New Year's Eve slaying marks the end of a violent holiday season in the Tacoma area."

Reading the faded article, I was trying to recall a visual in regard to who it could be. The murder was on the Hilltop, so it had to be gang related. Reading further, we did in fact have the male shooting victim at Region 5 Learning Center. As his crooked smile entered my visual memory, remembering him well, it was PT.

PT could have been a poster child for why smoking marijuana should never be legalized. At age fifteen, PT was mentally blown out. I am sure that at an early age gang members thought that it would be real funny to get little PT stoned on pot. As a result, PT had the twenty-four/seven look of a stoner and his quirky mannerisms reminded me of the flexible slinky character Gumby.

With a constant half-baked, practically closed-eyed look on his face, PT's body moved in unexpected directions. Sadly, his mental responses were similar to a light bulb that was flickering on and off as the result of alternating currents. It was difficult for him to focus on a particular subject for any length of time.

When PT first arrived at Region 5, we made several reports to his probation officer that he was coming to school stoned. The weird thing was that PT's urine analysis tests consistently came back clean. We just accepted the fact that he looked stoned but was not. He was all smiles and not an evil guy.

At Region 5 Learning Center we had a life sports program that the students could earn their way into. PT wanted to be a part of the program from the beginning. Simple things like consistent attendance, good work completion, and no suspensions or expulsions earned students the right to be in the program.

Without a gym at Region 5 Learning Center, our life sports program used a State of Washington passenger van to travel from location to location. The life sports program used the Al Davies Boys and Girls Club; and the Metropolitan Park District's outdoor recreation facilities as a classroom. Under the guidelines of the Washington State Juvenile Rehabilitation Administration, I could transport up to fifteen students at a time. It was a fun program and there was always a waiting list of students wanting to be a part of the activities.

For safety purposes, after lunch, quietly, I would inform our secretary as to where we were going for life sports, never telling the students our destination. I did not want gang members to call their buddies to "head us off at the pass" for a gang rivalry pay back. At the time, Region 5 had gang members from the Crips, Bloods, Disciples, and other associations all mixed into one little schoolhouse. With the gang rivalries at their peak in the late 1980s and 1990s, Region 5 sometimes seemed like a day at the O.K. corral.

The first thing that "the platoon," that's we called ourselves, would do was run a mile nonstop. Some students would start off running every other block and building up to a mile nonstop. It may seem like a simple task, but their pride at this accomplishment was immense.

PT had trouble from the start. His efforts to run the mile nonstop were so impressive that I just could not kick him out of the program. I suspected that after smoking so much weed, his body still reacted as if it were stoned. Being a long-distance runner and track coach, PT's running style was painful to watch. Even in distress, PT had a continual stoned look on his face. I can still recall coaching him saying, "Just keep it up. You will get it one day."

PT's big accomplishment happened one sunny afternoon on the Tacoma Ruston Way waterfront. On this particular day, we started our run from the old Asarco copper iron ore smelting plant and ran along the waterfront on the sidewalk. At the half-mile point, we turned around and ran back to the van. As usual, PT was last, but this time he did not walk once. In amazement, we watched and cheered him to the finish—he'd finally done it.

The mile was a run of honor; if you refused to run, you were out of the program. I used the mile run to weed out the punks. As the program evolved, the non-stop mile run was a badge of accomplishment and pride. PT had earned that badge and beamed.

At Region 5 we also exposed our students to camaraderie and team-building activities. Similar to running, basketball and volleyball were the same for PT, awkward. Just like the flexible Gumby character, one could never predict where PT's body parts were moving to or what he was going to do next.

In basketball nobody wanted to cover him, so guess who got the duty? My body paid the price—knee knocking, exchanging elbows to the body, and an occasional head butt kept me alert. Nothing really bothered PT. He was generally happy and had a positive attitude.

As with most students, when PT left Region 5 Learning Center, we did not hear from him again. Unlike other regular education teachers, we did not get invited to graduation ceremonies, weddings, or get Christmas cards in the mail.

The last thing that I'd heard about PT was that he had gotten out of prison, out of the gangs, and was married.

Before reading the article and realizing that it was PT and his wife shot dead on New Year's Eve, I had hoped that maybe there was life after the gangs. I guess in PT's situation, the urban legend was true: The only way out of the gang, is to die your way out.

As of this date, the evil murder of PT and his wife is still an unsolved homicide.

Man, woman found dead in idling sedan

HILLTOP: VEHICLE WAS LOCKED; DRIVER'S FOOT WAS ON BREAK

BY JASON HAGEY   **JANUARY 1, 1999**

The News Tribune

A man and a woman were found shot to death Tuesday evening inside a locked car that was idling in gear in the middle of an intersection in Tacoma's Hilltop neighborhood.

Police theorized that a third person shot both victims from inside the car and then fled, but there were no witnesses, said a Tacoma police spokesman.

The driver's foot was resting on the break when officers arrived shortly after 6:30 P.M., and at 9 P.M. the car was still idling in the street with its headlights on as investigators poured over it.

"It's a real different (crime), but I'm sure in the end there will be some kind of explanation, a police spokesperson said.

Investigators do not suspect a murder-suicide.

The identity of the victims hasn't been confirmed late Tuesday, but several people who gathered in the neighborhood said they believe they knew the victims' names.

Police wouldn't immediately let any of the people in the crowd close enough to the car to identify the victims.

People in the street described a bright young mother who became involved with the wrong crowd, and said the slayings probably were connected to drugs.

"She was a good kid," said a man who may be the grandfather of the young woman.

Another man who said he knew both victims called the slayings a tragedy that shouldn't happen, and he mourned the growing death toll that he attributed to drugs.

"The young lady that's in that car, she's a beautiful woman," he said." She's a scholar."

An anonymous caller phoned police about 6:30 P.M. to report that a car with two bodies inside was idling near South 17th Street and Grand Avenue.

It was obvious to the first officers on the scene that both victims were dead, he said. Investigators placed blocks in front of the tires of the 1989 Dodge Dynasty, but didn't immediately open the car doors.

The New Year's Eve slaying marks the end of a violent holiday season in the Tacoma area, punctuated by the Thanksgiving Day slaying of a 5-year-old boy and a 19-year-old woman.

Police have reported no arrests in the Nov. 28 shooting, in which they believed a gunman fired through a low-level window of a split-level home in Tacoma's South End.

6. Thrasher

After stumbling across the article about PT and his wife's assassination on New Year's Eve; I happened to find another article. This article had been securely tucked away in a running journal that I had kept in the 1980s. Keeping a running journal since the age twelve, it was only natural to also keep a diary of other activities in my life.

Collecting dirty laundry from my closet, I spotted my red *Runner's World* diary half hidden under the pile of clothes. Picking up my diary, a faded news article slithered out onto the bare wood floor. Sizing up the neatly folded article, I noticed an aged non-sticky strip of yellow tape attached.

Pausing before picking up the article, I wondered, "At one time the tape strip held the article safely tucked away. Why did it come loose now?"

Reaching for the article, an eerie thought passed through my mind. "Which dead student from Region 5 Learning Center wants out now?"

Opening the article and reading it, a student named Thrasher cleared the confusion in my thoughts. As his image materialized in my mind, I recalled that he'd come to Region 5 after moving from the California area with his mother.

Thrasher was not his real name—he earned the nicknamed during one of our life sports basketball games. During that game and many others, he proved to everyone that he was the best basketball lay-up driver in the platoon. He could thrash through several of us with ease and score at will. As a result, he became known as "Thrasher."

In a twist of fate, moving from California to the Tacoma School District in the middle of the semester meant that Thrasher could attend a regular school, but could not earn any credits. This was generally suggested to the students that schools did not want to work with. A counselor at one of the Tacoma high schools suggested that he attend Region 5.

For all we knew, Thrasher could have been a court-connected gangbanger from California. As it turned out, he showed no signs of being a criminal. Enrolling him, I was surprised that he was even referred to us. He was a very positive student, easy to work with and had a consistent smile. Thrasher did not make a single negative comment about our strict anti-gang dress code or behavior contract.

It turned out that Thrasher's mother moved to Tacoma to get married. As a result, Thrasher acquired a new stepbrother named Odie. Eventually, he and Thrasher both attended Region 5 at the same time.

When the second semester arrived, we suggested to their mother that she enroll Thrasher and Odie at a regular education high school. She refused and explained to us that she liked the structure, discipline, and activities offered at Region 5.

One of the Life Skills activities that Thrasher and Odie took was a 1.5-mile hike to "the saddle" between Pinnacle and Plumber Peak. Pinnacle Peak is located on the Tatoosh Range of the Cascade Mountains across the valley from the historic Paradise Inn. The Paradise Inn is located within the boundary of the Mount Rainier National Park.

The objective of this particular excursion was to study the tectonic plate movements of the Cascade Mountains. My "educational moment" was to show students firsthand the effect that tectonic plate movements had on mountain ranges.

After a 1.5-mile hike to the saddle between the peaks, it is easy to see the Sawtooth Mountain Range. The Sawtooth Mountain Range is a vivid example of tectonic plates pushing over one another creating a jagged landscape.

As usual, I took pictures of the students hiking, eating lunch, group pictures and individual snapshots. Once back at school, making a new photo-road trip poster, I stapled it up on the school wall for everyone to see.

Several years after Thrasher attended Region 5, he and his mother paid us an unexpected visit after school one day. In my classroom, I recognized Thrasher's voice. Quietly listening, I recall not hearing the echo of laughter penetrating the hall toward my classroom that usually accompanied his conversations. Leaving my classroom and following the sound of his voice, I approached Thrasher, took his right hand, and gave him a man hug.

Transfixed in the moment, I was caught off guard. For some reason, Thrasher held the embrace just a little longer than usual. Breaking the embrace, I had an odd feeling that something was wrong. We spent time exchanging small talk and joked about the basketball, volleyball, and pickle ball games we'd played. Of course, I rubbed it in, "You never did beat me in pickle ball."

Not laughing, Thrasher got a serious look and said, "Odie is dead."

Pausing with penetrating eye contact, holding back tears, he said, "Odie was gunned down like a dog!"

As he began reliving the evil events, I recalled reading the article in the newspaper. Sadly, at this point, so many former students had been shot or killed by drive-by shootings, Odie's evil murder did not stand out as anything unusual.

Interrupting my private thoughts, Thrasher continued, "Odie was gunned down in an apartment complex over a dumb argument he had at a gas station!"

As he was telling the story, slowly shaking my head, I could not help but think, "Another good man down." Odie and Thrasher were just fun-loving guys.

After a pause, Thrasher asked, "Can we have some pictures of Odie?"

Perplexed, I asked him, "What do you mean?"

"We don't have any school pictures of Odie for his funeral."

Overwhelmed by sadness, I told him, "You can have as many photos as you want."

It did not take us long to find the Pinnacle Peak poster board and the pictures of us smiling as we stood on the saddle between Pinnacle and Plumber Peak. Looking at the photos, absent-mindedly I said, "I was twelve years old when I first climbed to Pinnacle Peak with my dad."

Not sure why it came out, it was one of those thoughts that pop up and you cannot keep control of it. I recall being sad that Odie, as my father had done with me and as I do with my kids, would not be able to pass life's simple treasures onto his kids.

Thrasher appeared to be caught up in his own thoughts and did not respond. As we were looking at the poster board, a feeling of deep loss emanating from him. Instinctively, giving him a side-hug, I got a chair and a staple puller to disconnect the poster board from the wall.

On the wall, the vacant space where the photo poster board had been, left behind a lonely hollow shadow.

Giving Thrasher the entire poster board, he did not have to express his appreciation, I could feel it. Before he left we shook hands, had a man hug, and exchanged a moment of eye-to-eye contact. I could see in his eyes, as he could see in mine, we both felt the same way: what a waste.

Gunfire wound claims man's life

BY STACY BURNS   **JUNE 7, 1999**

The News Tribune

Sophie Ferdinand tightly gripped Odie King's hand, tears streaming down her face.

The 20-year old South Tacoma woman was nearly speechless as she watched King, her finance, lying unconscious in a hospital bed Saturday night with a gunshot wound to his head. Ferdinand remembers telling King, the father of her three children, that she loved him deeply.

Less than 30 minutes later, King 24, died. He had been shot in the head during a dispute while helping a friend's mother move in Lakewood that afternoon.

"I was his first love and he was my first love," Sophie said. "I am just glad I got to hold his hand."

Before King died, Pierce County sheriff's deputy arrested a 19-year-old man in the shooting and booked him into Pierce County Jail on suspicion of attempted murder.

"It's a senseless crime," said Vicki William, a friend who has known King for 10 years. "Now he's gone."

Friends and family describe King as a kindhearted family man who served as a role model to kids in his South Tacoma neighborhood. He loved to barbeque and play video games.

King moved to the Tacoma area from Los Angeles when he was 14. He lived with his parents on the East Side.

"King would help anybody," Vicki said.

Friends and neighbors say he was a peacemaker. King's friends wonder how a minor argument King got into Saturday afternoon turned deadly.

The dispute between King and the 19-year-old man started at a gas station in the 8400 block of South Tacoma Way about 3 p.m. King and a friend noticed the 19-year-old and another man in a nearby car giving King dirty looks, said Sophie, who spoke with King's friend after the shooting.

"That's how innocently it started," she said.

After a short conversation with the strangers, King and his friend left the station for a town house In the 8200 block of 29th Avenue Court South, where the two men were helping a friend's mother move into a new home.

Once there, King and his friend saw the men from the gas station. The 19-year-old lived in an apartment complex next door.

Again, the two strangers and King exchanged words, Sophie said. After a few minutes, King and the man with the 19-year-old stopped arguing. But the 19-year-old went into the nearby apartment and got a gun, deputies say.

"They were making amends," Sophie said "He (King) started walking away…"

Then King and his friend heard the 19-year-old cock his gun. "Everything went so fast," Ferdinand said.

A single bullet hit King in the head.

Friday, she said, King had talked about planning the couple's wedding.

"He gave me a kiss and told me he loved me," she said through tears.

Why do evil things like this happen?

Through the years, I have asked myself that question many times. Where does fate or God fit into this? Odie was a gentle man, described as a "peace-maker." Not remembering him saying a mean word to anyone, he was quiet and stayed to himself.

In despair, I have to wonder, what are the chances that the nineteen-year-old that Odie argued with at a South Tacoma gas station, happened to live in Lakewood?

Even more disturbingly coincidental, Odie's murderer, the gunman, lived right next door to where he and a buddy were helping another friend's mother move in. South Tacoma Way and Lakewood are miles apart.

I do not get it!

7. Bounced Out - Fell Into

Before falling into the position at Region 5 Learning Center, I almost quit teaching and had thought about going into real estate sales with my father.

Having the perfect teaching job at the same high school that I had graduated from, Wilson High School class of 1978, I was teaching life skills to special education students and was the head cross country coach and assistant track coach—life was good.

My being a coach was an added benefit for the shy special education students. Using the track and cross country athletes as my student assistants was a great experience for both the special education students and the athletes. The student assistants were required to eat lunch with the students and walk with them in the halls at least three times a week. At first the student assistances were reluctant, but over time they found it very rewarding to extend their tutorial duties beyond the classroom to help the students feel accepted.

Out of sight and tucked away in a distant corner of the school campus, my special education classroom was located next to the auto and small engine repair shop classes. Periodically, I would have to stop my instruction to wait for a car to stop revving its motor or for a repaired lawnmower being tested. It was hardly an ideal educational environment for my students having to stop instruction or shout to be heard.

Being young and unaware of the political hierarchy of the Tacoma School District's buddy system, I explained to the department head, "Wilson High School is out of compliance with Federal Special Education requirements for access to an equal learning environment."

Giving me a flat-line response that I do not recall, no action was taken.

Several weeks later, going to the next level, the vice principal barely showed a concern.

Undeterred, meeting with the principal, more a politician than anything—no assistance from him either.

Frustrated, venturing to the Tacoma Schools Central Administrative building located in downtown Tacoma, meeting with the head of Special Education Services, we had a real nice chat, but nothing changed.

At one point, the revving motors were so loud that during my January teacher evaluation, I was marked down for having a noisy learning environment. I was also marked down for having a coffee pot in my classroom. "Wow, huge violation!" I felt like screaming.

I recall trying to explain to the principal, who barely acknowledged my presence, "The staff lounge is too far away for me to get coffee." I also informed him, "I never go to the staff lounge anyway."

Pausing, knowing I was talking to the wall, I impressed upon him, "I am the only teacher that eats lunch with the students."

As if I had not uttered a word, in a monotone voice he repeated, "Rules are rules."

Failing to stare me down, looking away first, he got up and left. Frustrated, I kept my coffee pot and continued to eat lunch with my students in the cafeteria.

I wrote an appeal requesting that my negative teacher evaluation be amended. Never contacted, and I am not sure it ever was.

Throughout the year, tolerating the automotive and small engine disruptions, no action was taken. I dealt with it the best that I could. I loved the students and could see huge gains in their acquisition of knowledge and life skills.

In May, one morning before the students arrived, without warning or a phone call, the principal, whom I rarely saw, dropped by my classroom. Without a word he dropped a letter with a bold forest green Tacoma Schools letterhead at the top left corner on my desk.

Surprised, unable to decipher the upside-down letter, I asked, "What's this?"

His cold response was simple, "There are not enough special education students in the program to support another teacher." As he turned and walked away, he blurted out, "You're displaced."

Stunned, I recall thinking "What the heck!" I had not seen this coming at all. It was like the slow-motion movement of an impending car wreck. "Bam!" I was done. My teaching career at Wilson was over.

As I sat shell shocked, I figured it out. They were all connected. All the way up the chain of command, they were all "buddies." In reflection, all I did was try to get the best learning environment for my students. What did I get in return? I got ousted. I was sick to my stomach and to this day ponder the evilness of that administrative decision.

At the end of the school year, I was done. "Screw this," I thought. "Do your best and get canned, I don't think so!"

About six months later, out of the blue, my stepmother called and told me that a friend from Remann Hall Juvenile Detention Center knew about a job at a place called Region 5 Learning Center. I recall thinking, "What kind of crazy school is called Region 5?" My stepmother was unaware that I was mad and done with teaching. Looking for other work at the time, I was substitute teaching to earn enough money to hit the hills and snow ski.

"Well," I said to my stepmother, "who gave you the tip?"

The phone was silent for a moment. "Darrell, I was told not to tell you."

Now I was interested.

Out of curiosity, calling Tacoma School District's Central Administration building, after identifying myself, I asked about the position at Region 5 Learning Center. "There is no such position," said the person on the other end of the phone.

Pausing, I went on. "Whom am I talking to?" I do not remember her name, but responded, "I know for a fact that there is an opening at this place called Region 5." As calmly as I could, I explained. "I am a displaced teacher, and I demand an interview." I added, "Do I have to call my union?" At the time, I had no idea where the union building even was.

After a long silence, I could almost sense that the speaker button was being pushed to the on position for the gathering crowd. "Hold please," she said. "Mr. Hamlin, it appears that you are correct. Can we set you up for an interview?"

A week later, I was on 19th and Tacoma Avenue South in front of a small cinderblock building. The building, with a huge disconnected four-car garage in the rear, seemed odd. "What is this place?" I recall wondering.

Wearing a necktie and the nicest clothes I had—a clean pair of Levi 501 button-ups and an ironed shirt—I was ready to interview for a job that I did not really want.

My expectations of a formal interview were not what I received. The interviewing team of teachers were as relaxed and low key as they get. I remember that halfway through the interview, paused, I jokingly asked, "Can I take my tie off and get down to business?" Liking the staff from the beginning, I felt very comfortable with them. To this day, I can recall thinking, "What a great bunch of people."

I was still not interested in the job. Losing my dream job at Wilson High School, I did not visualize myself working with juvenile parole and probation criminals. It could have been my ego, I'm not sure.

Getting up from the interview and looking around, I felt that they must have sensed my disinterest. I could see the disappointment on their faces; we got along very well during my interview.

Making my move for a quick exit, Margaret, the director of Tacoma's alternative education sites, sensing our thoughts eased the tension by asking, "Would you like a tour?" With a polite nod, we were on our way.

Touring the U-shaped interior of the square cinderblock building, I recall thinking, "I could never work enclosed in a box like this—it's a trap."

"This would be your room," said Margaret as we entered a small windowless room at the end of the building. "No windows, no way!" were my thoughts at the time.

When we left the classroom and went out the rear emergency exit, it felt as if we were being released from a solitary confinement prison cellblock.

Once outside, without saying a word, Margaret headed for one of the garage doors. Having trouble with the lever, out of politeness, I gave assistance in lifting the heavy wood door. Behind the door was a dusty dull orange Department of Juvenile Rehabilitation Department sixteen-passenger van.

"What is this?"

Sizing me up, Margaret said, "I want more activities for our court-connected students, and I feel that with the right person, this van could get a lot of use."

"Who else uses it?" I asked.

Margaret in a disappointed voice replied, "No one."

Never taking my eyes off the van, I asked, "I can go on field trips?"

Without looking, I could sense a sneaky grin when Margaret replied, "You can do anything you want to help kids, but if you break the law, you're on your own."

I could tell when I turned to look into her eyes that she knew that she had me. But, I never forgot her warning: "If you break the law, you're on your own."

Taking the job, I wore out four different vans over a fifteen-year period. Being a turning point in my life, Region 5 Learning Center is one of the best blessings of my life.

8. Basics

Given the volatility of our court-connected students, Region 5 Learning Center was a small school. We were the halfway house for court-connected students coming out of Pierce County's Remann Hall Detention Center and the Washington State juvenile prisons.

Our goal was to get students that were released from the institutions ready for a regular classroom setting. Returning to regular school was not a given "right" for students on parole or probation, they had to earn their way back.

At Region 5 Learning Center, we had four teachers, a Paraprofessional, and a secretary. The maximum number of students enrolled at one time was supposed to be fifty, but generally we ran with more.

As the new teacher, I was known as the "rookie". Lucky for me, Leona, our secretary at the time, took me under her wing and kept me out of trouble with the Tacoma School District.

Leona also took very good care of the students at Region 5. She made sure student's lunch forms were properly filled out and bent the rules now and then to ensure students had bus passes to travel safely back and forth to school. At the time, just walking home from school with the wrong color clothing could get you shot or beat up.

Leona was the "mother hen" over all of us. She was the glue that held us together when things got crazy.

In 1985, Tacoma Schools was leading the state in developing unique alternative education programs trying to meet the needs of alternative learners, including Region 5 students on parole or probation. Being spread out across the Tacoma school district, there was only one principal for six different alternative education sites and the alternative high school. The lead teacher per program, were managers and acting administrator in emergency situations. But, without the help of secretaries like Leona, Region 5 could never have functioned smoothly.

In regard to my educational curricula, Moressa, who was the lead teacher, asked me to teach English. Pausing to size me up, she then asked, "What else do you want to teach?" Never been asked what I wanted to teach before, I found it refreshing.

"I like studying law and court cases. That would probably be perfect with this group," replying with an arrogant smirk.

Ignoring my insensitive comment, I recall that Moressa did not respond to my jesting. Looking through me, she curtly responded, "We have some *You in the Law* books. I suggest that you take a look at them," and walked away.

Aware that I'd offended Moressa, the experience of being asked what I wanted to teach was still very empowering. When I became lead teacher of Region 5, I also asked new teachers the same thing. "What do you want to teach?" It makes sense—if teachers taught the subjects they liked, they would be more excited about the subject matter.

After several weeks of developing and presenting my English and You in the Law curricula to the students, I was shocked at how low their academic levels were. I did not know if the students were lazy or just absent from school a lot. They did not know the simplest of things. Capitalization, punctuation, and spelling were ignored or unknown to them. Even to this day, I wonder how students can get through the American educational system and not know how to read or write properly.

Taking my concerns to Moressa, as always, she listened patiently. She was about five foot two and one of the bravest women I have ever met. I have witnessed her defuse dangerous gang situations with just the pointing of her finger. She had earned the respect of the students, and when she spoke, they listened.

In frustration, I explained to her, "How can I teach if these kids cannot read or write?"

Meeting my eyes with patience, she calmly said, "I guess it's your job to teach them."

Feeling the dagger straight to my heart, I popped off without thinking, "Yeah, sure."

As Moressa began addressing my snappy comment, I was listening and yet at the same time an echo from a friendly voice emerged from deep inside my subconscious slightly muffling her words. A best friend and teacher, Tim Shaffer, with whom I'd graduated from high school, once told me, "I trick them into learning."

Only catching bits and pieces of what Moressa was saying I nodded. "You're absolutely right."

To this day, I am still building academic curricula that trick students into learning. At the time, not knowing the skill level of court-connected students, I was very frustrated. I had it in my mind that every student deserved a traditional high school education. On many occasions during the first few years at Region 5, I had verbal phone battles with vice principals and counselors to accept our students back into the regular schools.

Amazing how little I knew.

In my heart, I knew Moressa was right; it was my job.

Starting with the basics and built from there, I tossed out individualized student instruction and went with whole group instruction. I graded students based on individual performance. My special education experience at Wilson High School taught me that whole group instruction helps raise the academic levels of the entire group.

Regarding my "You in the Law" curricula, I was shocked that students did not know great American heroes like Thurgood Marshall, Rosa Parks, or Linda Brown. Our students knew very little about search and seizure rights, probable cause, First Amendment rights, obstruction of justice, or the right to remain silent.

When explaining to people that I taught law to parole and probation students, they criticized me for teaching about the judicial system. One of the frequent comments was, "You're just creating jailhouse lawyers." I disagree.

From a young age, my mother taught me to believe that knowledge and education are the equalizers in America. As a result, I have always emphasized to students who have juvenile criminal records, "If you graduate from high school, get your GED or go to college, most people will not care about your past." I always concluded, "This is America, you get second chances."

After twenty-three years of teaching volatile court-connected students, I am still preaching that message: "Education is the equalizer in America."

It is interesting the journey our life takes. After absent-mindedly taking a right-hand turn at a red light instead of going straight, I became a secondary school teacher and a high school track and field coach. Putting to practice my educational curricula, I developed into a coaching teacher. As a coach, I know that the more we practice repetitively at something, the better our subconscious mind is at doing it. Working with academically delayed court-connected students, I learned quickly that the more consistent the curricula, the more consistent and successful the students will be.

Another challenge for our students was their inability to read the provided traditional grade level high school English textbooks. The average reading level of a Region 5 student was about fourth grade.

Struggling for weeks with the high school textbooks and feeling the same frustration as the students, I stumbled upon a cultural literacy dictionary with pictures. Our diverse student population knew very little about America or the people who had created our great nation. The cultural literacy dictionary that I stumbled across gave brief explanations of people, places, and events.

We started from scratch and built our English skills and history knowledge of America together; I was proud of their academic accomplishments.

9. Gambling Man

After developing appropriate academic curricula, I was still overwhelmed. I felt like something was missing. Then weeks later, a little voice directed me to open the mystery door, and I discovered the potential of our computer center.

In the middle of the U-shaped structure of our school, across from the men's bathroom, there was a windowless room rarely used. Resembling a cave, I found sixteen Apple IIe computers stashed away. The computer center turned out to be an academic gold mine.

For some reason during my tour of the Region 5 building, Margaret had neglected to show me the computer center. Or maybe, I was so caught up in establishing the life sports program and the road trips that I did not notice it.

Once discovered, I spent days searching through hundreds of floppy disk computer programs trying to find non-intimidating basic academic level building lessons. Finally, I narrowed it down to five basic computer programs that were not too difficult, but were still challenging.

Gambling Man was one of the spelling builder games that I stumbled upon. Once the disk was inserted, the image of an old western-style gambler would appear on the computer screen. Students were given a random amount of mixed-up letters and in a designated amount of time, had to make as many words as possible from the letters earning money.

When playing Gambling Man, the more sophisticated students would write as many words down as possible on a piece of paper before placing their bet. The more words typed, the more money they would win.

The students loved Gambling Man and without knowing it, they were tricked into improving their spelling skills.

To create more of a challenge, we would have Gambling Man competitions. The student, who could create the most words and win the most money, would earn a prize.

Another "trick the students into learning" computer program that I came across was Word Grubber.

Similar to the video game Ms Pac-Man, students gained points by grubbing words instead of dots. At the top of the screen students would be given a word, and in the boxes below were words that sounded similar to the word given and words that did not. As the students grubbed words that sounded similar they earned points.

Challenging the students as they were grubbing words as fast as they could, were grub monsters trying to grub them. Word Grubber was one of the favorite programs for the students and staff.

Surprisingly, my reading skills also improved by playing Word Grubber.

In regard to my English curricula, the most effective program that I found almost got tossed into the garbage. As I was organizing and cleaning the unused computer center, a matching definitions disk with no protective sleeve and a blank label fell to the ground.

Pausing, I thought, "Why did that happen?" Getting a weird feeling as I picked it up off the floor, I inserted the unmarked floppy disk into the computer. I discovered that I could adapt the program to our weekly spelling and vocabulary words. The nondescript program had a spelling and a matching definitions lesson.

At-risk students do not adapt well to change. Using the computer programs and other reading materials, I developed curricula that were consistent day after day, week after week.

As strange as it sounds, the most disruptive students would attend almost every day. I believe that it was the consistency of our program, positive atmosphere and a connection to Region 5 as "their" school that kept students coming back.

10. Weapons

From the sound of it, one might think that Region 5 Learning Center was a dangerous place to work.

There was always the chance that conflicts could erupt at any time, but I would like to believe that the students trusted us and felt safe. On many occasions students would warn us or give us a heads-up on a developing dangerous situation.

When I worked at Region 5, there was a persistent rumor around the school that students who were considered "gun slingers" ditched their weapons before coming into the building, purely out of respect.

Not knowing how true this really was, I would do unannounced locker searches sometimes twice a week as a deterrent. Complying with state statutes, if I searched one locker, I searched them all.

During the random locker searches, I moved their personal items around in their lockers, letting the students know that I was there. Given the amount of complaints received, I knew the searches were successful.

In fifteen years, I only confiscated one gun at Region 5. It was a lucky break.

One morning before school, a group-home student happened to see another student put a 22 caliber pistol in his locker. The gun slinger looked at the other student and said, "If you tell any-one, I'll shoot you!"

The threatened student had enough faith in the program that he told me in private about the gun. Not knowing how the situa-tion would unfold, I immediately notified the group home and had the student picked up.

Once in hand, I checked the gun cylinder to find two unspent bullets. Given all the shootings in Tacoma at the time, I wondered as I held the weapon, if it could have been used in a recent drive-by shooting. More disturbing, I wondered if the gun had killed someone.

Letting it pass, I called the police.

Before the police arrived, we silently signaled to each other an unannounced emergency building shut down. Once the police were in the building, the unsuspecting gun slinger was called out of his class for a fake phone call to be taken in the staff lounge.

Once in the lounge, he was searched, handcuffed, read his Miranda rights, and arrested by the Tacoma police.

As the gun slinger was being escorted by the police in handcuffs out of the building, we had the situation handled without the rest of the students ever suspecting a thing. Simply put, we closed our classroom doors and no one was allowed out until after the arrest.

Not a single student was aware of the events that had unfolded. That was the only gun incident at Region 5.

The gun slinger was immediately expelled and did not return.

11. Coffee Cup

After several weeks at Region 5, a student came up to me, looked around to make sure that no one was listening and said, "Do not leave your coffee cup lying around."

Puzzled, looking at the student, I asked, "What are you talking about?" Without saying a word, the student turned and walked away.

At the time, being a heavy coffee drinker, he must have noticed that I thought nothing of leaving my coffee cup unattended. Suspicious, I could not figure out what he was talking about.

Several days later I asked Rocko, the veteran teacher of Region 5, if he knew what the student meant.

Similar to me, Rocko had been displaced from one of the high schools after a disagreement with the principal. Tacoma Schools does not fire teachers or principals—they move them to another location.

I could relate to Rocko's situation after being bounced out of my dream job at Wilson High School. As time went on, I looked to him for advice as my mentor teacher and friend.

Rocko just looked at me and half laughed. "So you've finally found out." He explained, "The teacher before you was an excellent teacher and related well to the students."

Pausing to see if I was listening, he continued, "But, on one occasion, she was unexpectedly called out of her classroom to answer a personal phone call. While she was gone, one of the students walked up to her desk with his back to the class, unbuttoned his pants, and ran his private parts over the drinking surface of her coffee cup."

In a more serious tone he continued, "When she reentered her classroom, the student asked her, 'How do you take your coffee?'"

Expecting me to get the punch line, Rocko paused before finishing his explanation. "Without saying a word, she picked up her coffee cup, took a sip, and commented I like it black."

I recall being too stunned to respond and unable to visualize such an evil dastardly deed.

From what Rocko told me, the teasing from then on was relentless. She could not escape the daily harassment of those actions and asked for a transfer.

Strange that I owed my job to a student who took his "unit" out of his pants, ran it around the rim of a coffee cup, and relentlessly teased my predecessor out of her job.

To this day, I never leave my tea cup unsupervised.

12. Fluffy Light Pink Sweater

I was very naive when I started teaching at Region 5 Learning Center. Having no idea of the students' histories or their crimes, at the time, I did not care. The following is a recollection of one of many incidents that still haunts me to this day.

In the beginning, most of the students who attended Region 5 were court-connected males. It was rare to have a female in attendance. I do remember one female student in particular named Ellen who wore a fluffy light pink sweater.

The sweater I vividly remember, but her face I do not. As I recall, she reminded me of my first girlfriend when I was thirteen years old. Ellen had long brown wavy hair, brown eyes, and a warm smile. She was quiet, stayed to herself and was a pleasant person who wanted to learn new things.

I noticed that Ellen was dropped off and picked up daily by her parents, which was odd for Region 5. They never entered the parking lot in their shiny new white Cadillac; they always dropped her off at the curb, directly in front of the building. Being protective, the Cadillac did not pull away until she had entered the building safely.

The white Cadillac had tinted windows which I thought was unnecessary for a family vehicle. It was a nice ride, and I recall thinking that Ellen must have come from money. She was the only student who got dropped off and picked up daily by her parents.

Dissimilar to most of the students that attended Region 5, I thought that Ellen was pampered, assuming her crime must have been done to get her parents' attention. From the way she presented herself, she appeared to have everything. I also recall thinking that her loving parents must have been very protective, they were there every day on time to drop her off and pick her up. Out of curiosity, on several occasions, I tried to get a peek into the white Cadillac to catch a glance at her parents. Always parked and waiting on the busy street blocking traffic, she was in and out of the vehicle quickly.

Remembering quite clearly that she wore the fluffy light pink sweater more often than not, it appeared to be warm and cozy. The way Ellen presented herself when she wore the sweater reminded me of a child with her first blanket. In her case, the sweater fit snugly around her to keep her safe.

I imagined at the time that she may have gotten the sweater as a Christmas present from her grandparents and cherished it. She seemed more comfortable and at ease when she wore her fluffy light pink sweater.

It was hard to get to know Ellen. She rarely talked and did not attract attention to herself. Being attractive and well dressed, it was surprising that none of the boys ever hit on her for a date. It was odd—the boys did not mess with her at all.

I could tell by her writing skills that Ellen was smart. She could read well, write complete sentences, and use correct capitalization and punctuation. She buzzed through the assignments with ease and was doing quite well in class. She did her work every day and quietly left in the white Cadillac.

Then Ellen disappeared.

For several days after Ellen stopped attending school, there was something in the back of my mind that gave me an eerie feeling about her absence.

One afternoon when the students had left for the day, relaxing in the staff lounge I asked Rocko, "What do you think happened to Ellen?"

Rocko looked at me, tilted his head and said, "What do you mean?"

"Did her parents take her to Hawaii on a vacation or something?"

In a consoling fatherly voice, Rocko gently replied, "Rookie, she's a prostitute."

Shocked, I repeated, "A prostitute!"

In my mind, I could not visualize Ellen as a prostitute. My perception of prostitutes was that they were tough looking, addicted to drugs, and just plain rough.

As Rocko paused, taking in the magnitude of my ignorance, I sat looking down at the floor shaking my head in speechless shock.

Bringing me back to the normal momentum of time, Rocko went on to explain, "She probably went on the tour."

Regaining eye contact and remaining quiet, I was trying to come to grips with what I was hearing.

"Rookie, the pimps will take these young girls on the prostitution tour. They will take them from Tacoma to Seattle to Portland to San Francisco to Las Vegas and back to Seattle again."

I recall that Rocko's voice seemed to soften during his explanation as I absorbed what I refused to accept.

Curious, I asked, "Why do they do that?"

In a more serious tone to clear the fog from my head, Rocko responded, "Darrell, she's under age—if the pimps don't move their stable of young girls from one city to the next, they get busted."

"Stables, what do you mean stables?" I asked.

Looking puzzled, Rocko continued, "To the pimps, these girls are just property. They have no other value than to be sold for money."

In disbelief, I could not fathom that Ellen was involved in such a scary evil industry. To this day, I can recall the gentleness and kindness that emanated from her.

"What kind of monsters would prostitute out little girls!" I fired out in anger.

Rocko did not have a response. Looked at me, he shook his head, got up, and quietly left the room leaving me alone to ponder the evil that had unfolded in my reality.

13. Assaulted

During my twenty-three years as a learning specialist with court-connected students, I have only been assaulted twice. The first assault took place during a road trip and a tour under the Tacoma Narrows Bridge.

As a supplement to our Washington state history class, I showed the students a twenty-minute video of the Galloping Gerty. Galloping Gerty was the name given to the first Tacoma Narrows Bridge after it collapsed.

Before the video, I explained, "On November seventh, 1940, the wind ripping through the Tacoma Narrow's passage forced the steel girder constructed bridge to gallop like a wild horse. As a result, the bridge disintegrated." Continuing my explanation, "Rebuilding the bridge was a tricky situation. The Narrows Bridge was uninsured. The City of Tacoma paid eighty-seven thousand dollars expecting to have insurance on the bridge."

Pausing, to let the anticipation build, I concluded, "The insurance agent was so confident that the Narrows Bridge would never collapse that he kept the eighty-seven thousand dollars for himself without creating an insurance policy. After the collapse, the insurance agent disappeared."

Pausing, making eye contact to keep their attention, I continued, "The urban legend is that he skipped town for Mexico."

As I was explaining the details of the Narrows Bridge collapse and the juicy embezzlement story of the greedy insurance agent, Jessica raised her hand and asked, "Where is the Narrows Bridge?"

Jessica was a tough street girl who did not take guff from anyone. During her first week of attendance at Region 5, searching her purse one morning, I found a huge steak knife. Informing her that she was being suspended for having a weapon on campus, she just shrugged. She did not make up any excuses or put up the least amount of resistance. I found that odd.

Several weeks later, I had to suspend her again for having a rock in a long white tube sock. That suspension was a hard one to explain to her. Her explanation was that the rock in a sock was not a knife, so what was the big deal? I had to break the news to her that a rock in a sock was also considered a weapon.

As before, Jessica just shrugged, taking the suspension without another word for her defense. Not surprising, the rumor was that she was at Region 5 for stabbing someone. With a hollow expression regarding her suspension, Jessica just looked through me and said, "Okay."

Shocked by the question, I looked at Jessica and said, "What do you mean where is the Narrows Bridge?"

Embarrassed, Jessica in a shrill voice fired back, "Darrell, I have never seen the Narrows Bridge!"

By the tone in her voice, I could tell that I had touched a nerve. Seeing the anger seeping out and not wanting to humiliate her any further, I asked the rest of the class, "Has anyone seen the Narrows Bridge?"

In the back of my mind I was thinking, "I hope she does not have a rock in a sock now."

Not getting a response from anyone else in the class, I said, "Well, Jessica, it seems that other students have not seen the Narrows Bridge either." Quickly, I slipped the comment in to save face for the both of us.

"Jessica, tomorrow I am going to show you the second Tacoma Narrows Bridge and the remnants of the old Galloping Gerty."

With a puzzled look, Jessica responded, "What are 'remnants?'"

The next day for life sports instead of running our daily mile, I drove Jessica and several other students across the Narrows Bridge. The Narrows Bridge spans the distance from Tacoma across a narrow one-mile-wide saltwater channel toward Gig Harbor on Highway 16. As we were driving our JRA van across the Narrows Bridge, I lectured, "The debris field from the Narrows Bridge is larger than the debris field from the ship Titanic that sunk in April of 1912." I went on to explain, "As a result of the collapsed bridge debris field, the largest octopi in the world thrive right below us."

Interrupting, one of the students in the back of the van asked, "Is that the ship that flipped over?"

"No, that was a movie." I elaborated, "The Titanic on her maiden voyage sideswiped an iceberg and ended up sinking, killing one thousand twenty-four passengers."

"What is a 'maiden voyage?'" someone asked.

Over the student chatter, I blared back, "The first!"

Once across the Narrows Bridge, I took an immediate right turn and pulled underneath the structure of the bridge. Jumping the curb, I made a parking spot on the grass enabling us to exit safely from the van. I knew from previous explorations that there was a trail underneath the Narrows Bridge that would lead us down to the beach. It was a steep dusty hill and several of the students lost their footing getting their pants and shoes dirty.

Safely at the beach, searching under the bridge, we found broken cement with rusting metal rebar sticking out. Straggling out of the broken bits of cement, the bent rusting rebar resembled decaying skeletons marooned on a deserted beach. Pieces of faded green metal I-beams were also evidence that a disaster had taken place.

Relishing in the smell of fresh salt air, I had almost forgotten the reason why we were there. Looking at Jessica to get her attention and talking loud enough for everyone else to hear, I pointed and said, "Remnants are leftover pieces."

Squinting, as if interrupted from a trance, Jessica just shrugged and gazed back out appearing to be mesmerized by the quickly moving clear salt water.

Pointing up to the newer bridge structure, I said, "The previous bridge started flapping in the wind like a piece of paper in front of a fan." As I was explaining the theories of the bridge's destruction and waving my arm like a piece of paper in front of the moving blades of a table fan, we heard a loud "whoosh." To our surprise, a huge sea lion surfaced about twenty yards from the shore. Making eye contact as he leisurely swam by, pausing he curiously looked right at us.

As I pointed out the sea lion, several of the male students began throwing rocks trying to hit it. Startled, the sea lion made a weird expression of surprise, rotated his whiskery head, and disappeared.

I went ballistic, losing my cool I screamed at the rock-throwing fools, "You never throw rocks at animals." In a voice saved for extreme situations, I hollered, "I was raised to respect all life and that all life is important!"

In retrospect, most of the students attending Region 5 Learning Center did not have much respect for anything except their own need for immediate self-gratification.

Cooling down, more stern than angry, I explained, "You should never abuse animals."

Shamed for their actions, the rock throwers refused to make eye contact with me. I was happy to have gotten to their subconscious. Shame can be a powerful tool, if used correctly.

I explained, "All life is valuable—live, let live!"

Getting a weird feeling, I turned to see that Jessica was watching my every move. We met eyes for only a few moments, and with her hair wavering in the slight breeze, she barely nodded her head before returning back to peacefully gazing out at the slightly rippling clear green water.

As things settled down, to break the tension I asked, "How many of you can skip a rock across the water?"

Immediately, several of the tough guys picked up rocks and tried to skim them across the water with little success. Their attempts ended in huge plops.

Quietly kneeling down, I picked out a reddish rock and explained, "Flat rocks are the best." Without another word, turning toward the water, I flicked the flat rock. As it skipped six or seven times with the deescalating beat of my heart, I turned to make sure that they had observed my demonstration.

With their attention focused, I said, "On camping trips with my family, I have spent many days by rivers and at lakes attempting to get more skips across the water than my older sister. She had a much stronger throwing arm than I did."

Jessica, who was nearest to me, whispered to me with a distressed expression, "I've never skipped a rock in my life."

I thought, without saying out loud, "Amazing how many of life's little experiences these guys lack."

Looking at the group, I said in my teacher voice, "There is no better time than right now to learn how to skip rocks." Turning slightly, I quietly told Jessica the same thing that my mother always told me, "You can do anything you set your mind to."

After searching the beach, selecting a flat rock I demonstrated to Jessica and the other students who would listen, how to flick their wrists at an angle and force the rock to spin out of their hand.

Paying close attention to my demonstrations, Jessica reminded me of a little child trying to memorize a new trick. Seeing the excitement on her face, I found it hard to believe that she had never skipped rocks. At age seventeen, it was shocking that this was her first time driving across the Tacoma Narrows Bridge.

To make sure that Jessica's first rock skipping experience was successful, I selected a flat and round rock for her. Handing her the rock, I instructed, "Do as I do, follow my movements and I will stand right next to you."

As I recall, thinking that it would be safer not to stand right next to her, I moved down the beach about five feet or so.

I repeated, "Jessica, follow my every move."

Leaning over to skip my rock, I repeated again, "Bend your knees, lean over, and flick your wrist when throwing the rock."

As Jessica and I began to throw our rocks at the same time, I felt a "smack" to the right side of my forehead. Jessica in her excitement had released her skipping rock too late. The round flat rock hit me directly on the right side of my forehead.

With blood dribbling down the side of my face, I recall instantly trying to suppress pain and anger. No way would I ever cry in front of these guys. Managing my emotions and wiping the pain and the blood away from my face, I calmly locked eyes with Jessica and said, "Next time, please release your skipping rock a little sooner."

Seeing that Jessica was rattled, I calmly expressed to her, "I am fine. It was an accident."

Without speaking, immediately she showed a slight smile and an expression of relief.

Of course, some of the guys thought that it was funny and laughed out loud. One mad dog look from me gave them a clear message that this was not a laughing matter.

After the bloodshed, Jessica continued to practice and was thrilled to eventually be able to do a simple task like skip rocks across the water.

Sadly, as with Ellen who'd worn the fluffy light pink sweater, after several months, Jessica disappeared. I did not have to ask Rocko what happened to her.

In the small amount of time that Jessica attended Region 5, we all tried to expose her to a better lifestyle, a change. Jessica was rough and had a temper, but she was also a kind and gentle person once she trusted you.

Now she was gone.

14. Ferry Boats

Why road trips and life sports one might ask?

The urban legend I've mentioned before says, "You cannot take the kid out of the gang, they have to die their way out."

We believed that you can take the kid out of the gang. What I mean to say is, once out of Tacoma, up an unknown trail, miles into the wilderness, the gang ranks were dropped and camaraderie learned.

In regard to a need for a life sport program, one incident stands out. It happened on a clear afternoon when I took some life sports students to Tacoma's Point Defiance Park to play full court pickle ball. While there, an inner-city youth's perceptions shocked my reality.

The Point Defiance public park tennis courts that we used overlooked Puget Sound Bay. Puget Sound was named after Peter Puget who was an English explorer with George Vancouver. Peter helped George Vancouver map and claim for England the Puget Sound waters in 1792.

I told students that Puget Sound was named by George Vancouver after Peter fell into the salty cold water and almost drown. It is not an accurate story, but I was hoping that the visual would help them to remember who Puget Sound was named after.

The Tacoma area and the rest of Puget Sound have many islands and a ferry boat system to transport people and vehicles back and forth.

While in the heat of a pickle ball battle, Tyrone suddenly stopped playing. With a concerned look on his face he asked, "What are those cars doing on that boat?"

Once I quieted down the students from laughing, calmly I explained to Tyrone, who had lived in Tacoma for his entire life, "The green and white boat was called a ferry." Pointing across Puget Sound to Vashon Island, I went on, "The ferry boat system transports people and cars from island to island." I gently explained further, "The ferry system is similar to the bus system except that these buses float from place to place."

Listening intently, his eyes remained focused on the green and white ferry boat. By his expression, he seemed to stare in disbelief. Stunned, I thought, "Here is a seventeen-year-old who's lived in Tacoma his entire life who has never seen a ferry boat. Wow!"

How can we expect people to change if we do not expose them to positive healthy lifestyles? The huge challenge before us is how to modify disconnected crime-impacted student behaviors and get them out of their self-destructive crime cycle. Our goal was to expose crime-impacted students to a healthy alternative lifestyle and give them options.

Sadly, the only part of the beautiful Pacific Northwest that Tyrone had been exposed to was the confined concrete area of the low-income Hilltop.

The educational life skills program was designed to make a high-impact impression on inner-city court-connected students. Our hope was that by exposing students to a healthy lifestyle, they would, in turn, expose their children to similar activities. We were trying to break the generational cycle of crime and violence.

The first out-of-town road trip that I took with students developed quite innocently. After stabilizing my curricula and with the life sports program developing, I wanted to start the road trip program at Region 5 Learning Center.

One morning, I noticed one of our Native American students admiring the view of Mount Rainier while standing next to our security door. The Region 5 building on 19th and Tacoma Avenue South had a beautiful view of the Cascade Mountains and Mount Rainier. On several occasions, I remember admiring the sunrise while waiting to check students at the door for weapons and dress code violations.

On this particular day, as the sun began emerging over the Cascade Mountains in an array of beautiful colors, I happened to notice Nighthorse's reflection through the glass door. From my vantage point, off the reflection of the glass, I could see deep sadness in his expression.

Keeping a safe distance from him, I observed that he quickly swiped a tear from his cheek. Turning to glance around to make sure that nobody had noticed, we made eye contact. Looking away, I pretended not to notice the tears building. Crying at Region 5 would have meant relentless teasing.

Without making eye contact, I simply said, "What a beautiful view of Mount Rainier."

Without turning away from the view and the emanating colors of the sunrise, Nighthorse replied, "My grandfather always said he was going to take me there." Pausing to gather strength he added, "Now he's dead."

Pausing to let him have a moment, a few seconds later, I said, "Then let's go."

And that is how our Region 5 road trips to the Mount Rainier National Park and to other Cascade Mountain adventures began.

15. Punch Drunk

As our road trip adventures expanded, several times a year I would take the North Star Platoon hiking up to Lake Annette. Lake Annette is a beautiful alpine lake hidden about five miles into the Cascade Mountains. The trailhead is located just off of Interstate 90 going east toward Snoqualmie pass.

The name North Star Platoon emerged during one of our road trips. I do not remember when, but one day as we were hiking through the woods an apprehensive student asked me, "What do we do if we get lost?"

I explained to him, "Similar to the early explorers who walked twelve hundred miles to the Pacific Northwest along the Oregon Trail, we would use the North Star to set our bearings toward the next vantage point in the distance." From that point forward, we referred to ourselves as the "North Star Platoon."

Unconvinced by my explanation, as I recall, he stuck very close to me the entire hike.

It was Lammy who on a hike to Lake Annette counted thirteen switchbacks and complained every step of the way. A hiking trail switch-back occurs when the grade of the hike is too steep to walk up. The trail zigzags back and forth until the grade levels off.

Lammy was as huge as a red pop machine and just as hard to move. Waiting as he was resting, I told him, "When I was twelve, I hiked a heavy blue rubber raft up this."

"Is that supposed to help?" Lammy wheezed out. "You're crazy. We don't have mountains like this on the islands," he blurted out.

With much positive reinforcement, Lammy finally made it past the switchbacks and down into the valley to the lake. He was the only student that I know of to ever count the thirteen switchbacks and I believed him.

Similar to Lammy, new platoon members usually griped and complained the entire hike to Lake Annette. It was not until they completed the five-mile climb and were captivated by the beauty of the pristine aqua-colored lake that they quit complaining. Or maybe, it was that they were just too tired and hungry to complain anymore. To reach Lake Annette was quite the accomplishment.

Generally, after resting and eating our lunches, depending on the hiking conditions, I would give the platoon members a couple of minutes' head start back down the trail. As they were leaving, if I had the money, I would yell out, "Anyone who can beat me to the van gets a hot fudge sundae!"

Hearing this, the veteran platoon members never let on that they knew that everyone would be getting a hot fudge sundae regardless of getting back to the van before me or not. For them, it was a matter of pride and an honor to beat me down the hill.

Giving the platoon several minutes' head start back to the van also gave me some quiet time and the opportunity to police up the litter. Many times as they took off running, I remember yelling, "You're disqualified if you cut the switchbacks!"

On this occasion, as with many, several minutes after they took off running down the trail, I started running and screaming like a nut with my hair on fire.

Being a long distance runner, it did not take me long to catch two Eastside Bloods sitting down taking a break for water. I was quietly on them before they could put their water bottles down. "Gotcha!" I yelled, sprinting by tagging and bagging them both.

Continuing on, running along the trail and turning sharply on the switchbacks, I could see him. "Jackson, here I come!" I yelled.

Jackson was a Hilltop Crip and proud of it. He was notorious for sneaking into Region 5 his perfectly ironed blue bandanna and pager every chance he could. He was an instigator and a trouble-maker. Standing out like President Abraham Lincoln in an old Civil War photo, he was about six feet three inches tall and wore a huge afro hair style.

I was on him like a cougar on prey. "I got you," I proclaimed with an out-of-breath mocking tone.

As I tagged and bagged my third victim, I noticed that Jackson did not look right. At a glance Jackson looked punch drunk or stoned, I could not tell. Several steps down the trail a little voice began to speak to me. Rationalizing, I thought, "He looked weird, but if I stop now, I will never catch the rest of the platoon."

With an eerie feeling creeping into my awareness, I began listening to the little voice from the back of my subconscious saying, "Something's wrong." Listening to myself, I turned around and headed back up the trail for Jackson.

As I approached punch drunk Jackson, he stumbled and fell hard to the ground. I could tell immediately that something was not right.

Observing how he lackadaisically picked himself up, his knees were dirty. Twigs, dirt, and leaves were intertwined into his usually well-maintained afro. Worrying, I thought almost out loud, "Two miles and about seven switchbacks into the Cascade Mountains and Punch Drunk Jackson is out of it—now what do I do?"

Pausing to size up the situation, I thought back to when we'd left Region 5. He hadn't smelled of alcohol and I'd searched everyone before we left for pipes and weed. What was wrong with this guy?

"Jackson, what is wrong with you?"

"I forgot my medicine," he babbled.

"Medicine? what medicine?" I snapped back in a more concerned voice.

He sat down and gazed through the trees with a peaceful expression. Interrupting his trance, I sarcastically asked, "You don't see a bright light do you?"

Jackson calmly shook his head slowly and said, "I'm, I'm a diabetic."

I thought of a *News Tribune* headline: Tacoma School District student dies on trail, teacher held responsible.

Then my instincts kicked into gear. I tore into my backpack looking for some sugar—none! I'd shared my entire lunch with the platoon at the lake. Jackson was too big to carry down the hill, and by the time I ran to the van for assistance and came back, he might go into shock or die. For all I knew about his medical condition, he could have been dying right then.

Searching for a solution, looking up the switchbacks of the trail, I noticed the two Eastside Bloods and yelled, "Hurry up—we need your help!"

Once upon us, I could tell that the Bloods did not want anything to do with Punch Drunk Jackson. He was mean to them and an enemy.

I explained the situation as quickly and clearly as I could. They just looked at me with an expression that said, "Let him die."

"Look!" I yelled, getting their attention. "I need your help!" Keeping an eye on Punch Drunk Jackson I said, "I want one of you to run down the trail." Turning, I commanded the Bloods, "I want the other to run back up the trail."

With their attention focused on me and not their anger, I went on to explain, "You have to find some sugar. Any type of sugar will do. Find some hikers and explain to them that we have a diabetic emergency and need sugar." I could tell by the look in their eyes that they did not want to help a 23rd Street Hilltop Crip. I sensed that my request for assistance was not overpowering their feeling of hatred. Before any more hate spewed from their thoughts, I yelled, "Move it! This is for the platoon!"

Without speaking, they split off in different directions.

Watching the Eastside Bloods disappear, I said a little prayer and let it go.

Almost unconscious, Punch Drunk and I stumbled down the trail to a stream. He was a lot heavier than anticipated, and we almost stumbled to the ground several times. Finally making it, bending the rules, I let him drink water directly from the stream. Diarrhea from "beaver fever" was the least of my concerns.

It is interesting how in these types of crisis situations, time seems to slow down. It seemed forever before one of the Bloods got back to us. The Blood, totally out of breath, silently handed me a rice crispy crunch bar. As if not there, he made no eye contact with Jackson.

"How ironic," I recall thinking taking the colorful wrapping off the candy bar with a grin. "Snap, crackle, and pop is how the gang-bangers described the sounds of a drive-by shooting."

"Here, eat this quickly!" I ordered Jackson. While Punch Drunk was finishing the snap crackle pop candy bar, the other Blood showed up with a can of pop. I could sense that they felt good about rendering assistance, even if it were to a Crip. Through their expressions, I could see a glow about them for their success.

Patiently waiting for several minutes, glossy-eyed Jackson began to return to his cocky hotheaded Crip self.

"Okay, you two head to the van and explain that we will be there. Do not panic—we will be there."

Before the Bloods left running down the trail, I grabbed a shoulder of each, looked them long and hard in the eyes and said, "Thanks. You're good guys."

Punch Drunk did not say a word, not even a thank you.

As Punch Drunk began to get up for the remainder of the hike, I told him, "The Bloods from the Eastside saved your butt!"

Not responding, looking straight through me, he was either still in sugar shock or surprised. "Those red guys could have just run on by and let you die in the woods for all the grief you give them every day at school. I am surprised that they even bothered to help you at all!"

Letting my comments hang for a little while, I said. "Next time you give them grief, you better remember this." I was not abrasive; I was firm.

After about an hour, finally making it back to the van, thankfully we dodged another potential disaster.

Of course, the platoon was more interested in the winning of their hot fudge sundaes than in Jackson's near-death experience. In the end, without expressing it, we shared the same feeling of ease. The platoon was together again in the safety of our van.

After our hot fudge sundae stop in North Bend, as usual, almost the entire platoon fell fast asleep for the journey home. It was common after a long hike, mountain biking, or snowshoeing adventure for me to be the only one awake in the van. Tough guys, bullies, sex offenders, murderers, car thieves, burglars, and gangsters were usually all crashed out together. Some of the platoon members were leaning on each other and others had their heads touching as one. To be honest, it was odd to see everyone not arguing and at peace together.

Driving down Interstate 90 for home, I happened to looked up at the rear view mirror. Jackson was the only one awake. He was just gazing out of the window almost mesmerized by the landscape of the Cascade foothills. I remember thinking, "What is on your mind?" Then he caught me, and our eyes locked.

Expressionless as I looked at his mirrored image, I tried to wordlessly convey, "You're one lucky dude today."

Jackson just nodded and gazed back out the window. Not a word was spoken between us, but he knew my message.

After the insulin scare on the hike, Jackson did not give up the gangs. Really, what else did he have? One thing I did notice, after the hike, during school, Jackson rarely ever gave an Eastside Blood grief. He was not friendly, that would be against gang law, but he never went out of his way to bother the Bloods again.

16. Not Too Blue

About ten, maybe fifteen years after Punch Drunk Jackson's near-death experience, he unexpectedly emerged like a ghost from a distant past. As Region 5 occurrences were strangely becoming more frequent, I was hardly taken by surprise when he whooshed by me at Jefferson Elementary School where my daughter Kaylee was a student.

Recognizing him, he did not notice me. Jackson's hair was cut shorter, and he was not wearing too much blue. There was no neatly folded ironed blue bandanna hanging out of his right rear pocket, and he appeared to be pretty clean cut all around. There were no signs of gang affiliations that I could see.

Watching him stride toward the white metal fence of the kindergarten section of the school grounds, I caught myself wondering if he would remember me. Drawn toward him, I found myself following him from a discreet distance. Casually draped over the white protective fence, Jackson stood patiently anticipating the mad and exciting race of children to their parents' open arms.

Making sure he was not paying attention, stealthily, I moved right next to him intentionally invading his personal bubble just enough not to alarm him.

Uneasy and without looking toward me, Jackson moved a little. I moved toward him an inch closer.

Jackson looked over, took a glance down, and moved again.

Moving again, I invaded his comfort zone.

Saying nothing, looking down, not moving, expressionlessly, he turned away.

Turning for a final time, with a huge smile, he asked, "Where's your beard?"

"It was getting gray and everyone was asking me if my daughter was my grandchild," I said. "What are you doing?"

Jackson in a man's voice of maturity said, "I'm here to pick up my girlfriend's daughter."

"You look great, Jackson, and I see you're still alive when a lot of your buddies are dead or in prison."

Barely making eye contact he said, "I got out of that."

Interrupting our exchange and running with great excitement, his girlfriend's daughter jumped into Jackson's arms and giving him a huge I-love-you-Daddy hug.

As if watching a news clip, I felt like a bystander to the evolving events. Fighting off mental images of the gangbanger Jackson, I caught myself smiling. I was very impressed.

As Jackson held the little girl in his arms, he paid little attention to me. Our short conversation was over. I am not sure that Jackson even liked me very much.

Watching Jackson meander off, tall, clean-cut, and holding a little girl's hand, I thought, "He's not a bad guy after all."

Glad to see that Punch Drunk Jackson was still alive, I was caught wondering if other students from Region 5 had made it too.

17. King Salmon

started working at Region 5 Learning Center when I was about twenty-five years old. I think that I was twenty-five years old, "man time" is different from real time. Being married, I learned early that women and men have different interpretations of the value of time and dates. To confirm that theory, ask any man the date and year of his wife's birthday or their anniversary.

In the scheme of time recollection, "man time," I was in my twenties, young, single, and had no kids. Having a lot of free time, I found it rewarding to do special activities for the students.

Region 5 students had one of several factors in common that seemed to lead them into a path of crime. Not every student, but I would say that eighty percent of the court-connected students lacked a fatherly male influence. I have often wondered, if not for my father and grandfather, would I have ended up court connected?

One day in class, to personalize my relationship with the students, I was telling some Alaskan fishing stories of working on a salmon gillnet boat near False Pass, Alaska. After story time, a student surprised me by remaining seated.

Jake, who was generally a quiet student, confided in me, "I have never been fishing." He must have been embarrassed because he waited until everyone had left the classroom and spoke in a whisper sharing his regrets.

Face to face, I said, "Then let's go."

With our goal to go fishing in mind, I took Jake and two other students up to our family cabin on Ohop Lake one day after school. At the time, the cabin was a one-room structure with an old wood-burning Franklin stove for heat.

The previous summer my windsurfer had melted in a friend's house fire, and I'd applied the insurance money from it to build a new dock on the lake. Planning to eventually have children, I built the dock in an L-shape that provided protection for small children playing in the water.

Arriving at the cabin, the first thing I did was to get the guys set up with fishing poles and hooks. We found our own earthworms under a rotting piece of wood that was stuck in the moist dirt.

While on the dock, I explained to the boys, "The best place to catch fish is on either the right or the left side of the dock." Pointing off the front of the dock, I made it clear. "There is an old sunken cedar log about ten feet off of the dock."

Pausing to make sure they were listening, I continued, "It is a hook-snagging log. It is best to stay clear of it." I reminded the three of them, "I need to study for a class, and I will be in the cabin doing some reading while you're fishing. Do not get in the water!"

Settled in, I positioned myself at the front window of the little old cabin so that I could watch them fish while I read. Having one of them fall in and drown would bring a quick end to my teaching career.

After a bit of reading, noticing that the other two guys were digging in what was now a mud hole and playing with worms, I recall wondering to myself that maybe they had never played with worms before. Glancing over at Jake, I noticed he was fishing right off the front of my new L-shaped dock. I thought, "What a stubborn guy!" I'd been quite clear in my explanation of where the fish could be caught. In my pre-father mind, all I could think was, "Why didn't he listen?"

At that point, I made up my mind that if his hook got snagged on that old sunken log, he was on his own. I thought to myself, "That headstrong boy will never catch a fish anyway," and went back to reading.

Before long, immediately breaking my concentration, Jake gave out a yell that must have echoed all the way back to Tacoma. Looking up, ready to jump into action, I prepared myself for a rescue attempt. Noticing that Jake hadn't fallen into the lake, oddly, he was fighting with his pole.

"What is he doing?" I wondered.

Jake must have thought that he had a king salmon on the hook the way that he was fighting with the pole. Watching, I noticed that Jake took time out from the big fight, glanced back at the cabin, not much of a glance, but just enough to express, "Don't tell me where to fish!"

Returning to the catch, Jake started reeling and stepping back, reeling and stepping back.

"No way," I thought. "He has to stop. Oh no," I said under my breath.

As Jake was reeling and fighting for the first big catch of his life, he walked right off the back of the L-shaped dock. Splash he went.

I was out of my seat and down the hill in a flash. No way did I want to give this guy mouth-to-mouth resuscitation if I could avoid it. Before reaching him, Jake had stumbled out of the water soaking wet.

At first, not a single word was spoken. After a moment of looking at each other, in utter surprise, the four of us laughed almost until tears were rolling down our cheeks. We were all shocked to see that Jake, with pole in hand, still had the small lake trout on the hook.

In the end, Jake tossed his first small catch back into the lake.

"Live, let live," I told him.

After changing into dry clothes, barely able to keep an extra pair of my oversized pants on, Jake was all smiles and what a story he had to tell.

18. Bigfoot's Unit

Another funny incident with Jake occurred on a road trip several years after the eruption of Mount St. Helens on May 18, 1980. The eruption of Mount St. Helens was a catastrophic event and left massive destruction in its wake.

We were studying Washington state history, and I decided to take the students on a road trip to the Toutle River to investigate the damage done by the volcanic explosion. We drove south on Interstate 5 from Tacoma and took a left-hand turn at the Toutle River turnoff. Our first stop was the Toutle River museum and exploratory center. After wandering around the museum, we decided to drive further east up the river.

If I had to, I could probably find the location again. The once-productive motel, grocery store, and gas station were almost completely covered by the mud and ash that flowed out of Mount St. Helens. At about five hundred miles an hour, the flow of ash, trees, and other debris left a huge destructive impression on the area.

Walking across the street from the almost submerged motel to the Toutle River, scourging around, we found massive amounts of small pumice rocks. The lightweight milk-colored rocks were mixed in with the huge boulders that prevented the Toutle River from spilling out and over the two-lane highway.

The students were very surprised to find that the pumice rocks would float. I explained to them that pumice was cooked rock and had air bubbles inside that made it less dense than the water. They got a kick out of tossing the milk-colored rocks into the river and watching them float away. Floating rock is something you do not see every day. Skipping pumice rocks across the flowing river was an easy task; they were almost as light as air.

After collecting pumice rocks to take back to Region 5, we hustled back to explore the eerie abandoned mud-filled motel and gas station.

For reasons I don't recall, the only thing that seemed to survive the Toutle River ash and mudflow intact was a roadside attraction of Bigfoot. The Bigfoot statue must have been twenty-five feet tall and looked quite intimidating.

As Jake and I were investigating the Bigfoot statue, I suggested that we get a picture of him next to the monster. Jake, who had gone on many road trips, knew that I would make a photo-poster board for the Region 5 building and he was eager to comply.

The poster boards were very important to our students. Most of our students were probably not going back to the traditional regular school or graduate. As a result, they would not have the chance for a yearbook. With that in mind, I ordered doubles of the road trip photos. One set of photos went for the photo-poster board and the other set for the students. Our hope was that the photos would give students something positive to reflect back upon. After making the poster board, each student would be given the pictures in which they were the focal point.

Over a fifteen-year period, the photo-poster boards, which were stapled to the interior walls of Region 5, were a chronology of events and activities that we exposed students to. Often returning students would spend most of their time looking for their pictures on the poster boards, barely visiting with us.

The poster boards gave our students a feeling of connection. Most of our disconnected students did not have a positive experience in the traditional education system. The photo-poster boards brought our students closer together as a unified group and build a sense of community. Most of our students were a mismatched collection of kids that other schools refused to deal with.

In addition to building a community to identify with, and in an attempt to break gang barriers, it was empowering to take photos of opposing gang members working together. Being photographed together helped our students visualize that we were one race, the human race. The challenging adventures of the life skills program broke social barriers and tricked rival gang members into getting along.

On this day, only having a cheap yellow box camera to take Jake's picture, I had to stand back quite a ways to fit Bigfoot into the frame. Looking through the little camera viewfinder, Jake was between Bigfoot's legs as I snapped the picture. At the time, I recall thinking that it was odd that he was standing right between Bigfoot's legs and waving his hands. When taking the photo, I probably thought, "How nice of Jake to be waving."

The next day after getting the pictures from the one-hour photo processing store, eagerly, I created the group photo-poster board. The snapshot of Jake in front of Bigfoot did not stand out to me. Several group pictures, pictures of students picking pumice out of the river, and the usual individual road trip photos were taken.

Once I got the poster board stapled up on the wall so that everyone could see it, standing, back nothing peculiar stood out.

Admiring the poster board of our Toutle River exploration, Roman, another teacher approached. Pausing to gather the right words, pointing he said, "Jake is doing something inappropriate between Bigfoot's legs."

Roman was the force that kept me grounded. He was a practical thinker and a realist about the world. Roman was in charge at Region 5 when I was out of the building. We made a perfect team working together. Once, one of the teachers sarcastically compared us to James T. Kirk and Spock from *Star Trek*. Surprising the condescending teacher, Roman and I took it as a compliment.

Staring at the photos on the poster board, I could not figure out what Roman was talking about. With a puzzled expression, Roman looked at me and said, "Jake appears to be holding up Bigfoot's testicles."

To be honest, at first, I was disappointed that Jake would do such a thing. Now that it was pointed out to me, I could clearly see Jake holding up Bigfoot's private parts and laughing. Standing next to Roman in shock, the photo transformation reminded me of psychological test situation of a dual image in one. One interpretation is of a beautiful woman, who upon closer examination is a scary witch.

I said to Roman, "In my opinion, this is just another example of a fun-loving teenager getting one over on an adult."

Roman suggested the removal of the photo. Disagreeing, I explained, "If I did not detect Jake holding up Bigfoot's private parts, most likely no one else would either."

"Besides", I said, "That has got to be one of the funniest photos I've ever taken." As usual, Roman just shook his head and walked away.

To be on the safe side, I did not give the second copy of the Bigfoot photo to Jake. It is interesting, he did not ask for it either.

In the end, I did not confront Jake in regard to holding up Bigfoot's private parts. I was hoping that he would bring it up; he never did and I let it go.

The picture of Jake holding up Bigfoot's private parts went unnoticed and stayed on the hallway walls until an angry administrator retaliated against me. Not understanding the unique camaraderie power that the poster boards possessed, during one summer break, she dismantled the chronological history of student activities and haphazardly stacked them on my classroom desk.

In respect to the students who had passed through and survived Region 5, to spite her simple-minded vengeful actions, I stapled every one of the student photo-poster boards on my classroom walls.

19. Unnoticed

Several weeks after the Toutle River expedition, Jake slipped into my classroom early one Monday morning and whispered to me, "I saved someone's life."

"Yeah, right," I thought at first. Then I reflected back on the fact that Jake had shown great honor at Region 5 and seemed to be a man of truth. Unsure, I used my standard response to student's stories: "What do you mean?"

"I was having a water balloon fight with some friends and heard a woman screaming."

Looking around making sure no one could hear, he continued, "Following the screaming, I ran over, jumped the fence, and found a little girl on the ground." In a matter of fact tone, he went on. "She was lying on the ground all purple in the face."

"You're kidding," I said, "What did you do?"

With as serious a look as I have ever seen in those fun-loving eyes, he said, "I picked her up by her feet and slapped her on the back."

"Then what happened?" I asked, almost believing the story. "Who could make a thing like this up?" I thought in silence.

Hearing footsteps in the hall, looking around again to make sure no one else could hear, Jake said, "Like a bullet, a piece of hot dog shot right out of her mouth."

At this point, I recall being totally into the story. "What happened next?"

Almost relieved to be retelling his life-changing event, Jake said, "I jumped the fence and left." Jake paused and added as an afterthought, "Please don't tell anyone about this."

Having no memory of my response to Jake's story, I think he just turned and quietly walked away.

After school, calling the fire department near Jake's house, I was then directed to a central emergency dispatch department. They gave me the number to someone else. I remember that it was no easy task to find out whom to talk to in regard to the verification of Jake remarkable story.

Once connected to the right person within the emergency dispatch department, I explained Jake's life-saving adventure.

At first, the person on the other end of the phone was not too interested. Sensing being mentally disconnected from the other end, I began retelling Jake's story to make sure that there was a clear understanding of the facts. I recall picturing the person on the other end of the phone just bobbing their head up and down while chomping on a big wad of gun.

I caught myself being distracted visualizing one of the Seattle Mariner's bobble-head dolls that they give away on game night to attract little kids to a baseball game. It was becoming obvious that this person was not really paying attention. With the bobble-head doll visual in my thoughts, about halfway through telling the story the third time, pausing, I left a dead space in the conversation that could not be ignored.

After what seemed like minutes, I calmly asked, "By the way, I did not get your name. Do you have a badge number that I can refer to as well?"

I could almost visualize the faceless bobble-head sitting straight up in their seat. After more delay, the first question that

Bobble-head asked was, "What was the boy's name?" He also asked for Jake's address and phone number.

I was finally getting some action.

Having Bobble-head's name and badge number, several days later I called him back.

"I have been meaning to call you," was the first thing that Bobble-head said. They relayed to me that there had been an incident on the East Side of Tacoma, but it appeared as if the paramedics on the scene had handled the situation.

"Was a hot dog involved?" I asked quickly.

After a lengthy pause I continued, "They took credit for what someone else did."

I received more silence. Eventually, Bobble-head simply replied, "I will check and find out." Click.

Shortly thereafter, I received a verification call from Bobble-head that the paramedics came clean in regard to the hot dog. In a sheepish tone, Bobble-head relayed, "They confirmed that the piece of hotdog was dislodged from the little girl's throat before they arrived on the scene."

I simply responded, "I know exactly how that hot dog was dislodged from her throat."

Bobble-head fired back, "We will be back in contact with you." Click.

Next, I called *The News Tribune* and tracked down someone who was responsible for covering the Tacoma School District's newsworthy events. Excitedly relaying to the person on the other end of the phone the life-saving details, I got about the same flat-line response as I'd originally gotten from Bobble-head.

Somewhat frustrated I asked, "Are you going to interview Jake?"

"We will do what we can," was the response from the other end.

As usual, I asked for the person's name and direct phone number. In addition, I gave the appropriate emergency number and point of contact for verification with the Tacoma Fire Department.

Right before they hung up I asked, "Don't you want to know Jake's number and address?"

"Oh yes. I will need that information, won't I," they responded in a sarcastic tone.

After passing on the information, I was very excited for Jake. He did not expect any recognition for saving the little girl's life. Jake was a true hero.

Every morning for the next several days I waited patiently for the news from Jake that someone from *The News Tribune* had discovered his heroic actions. I mean, really, how often does a person get the opportunity to save another life?

As days passed, Jake gave no indication whatsoever that he had been contacted by the media. I was hot; how could this lapse of recognition have happened?

After school one day, about a week after having my conversation with *The News Tribune,* locating my documentation out, I hopped on the phone to track down the person I'd given Jake's story to.

I was abrasive and clear. "If Jake had raped or murdered the little girl, he would have been all over the front page!"

Emotionally I expressed further, "He does something good and you don't give a damn!" In my twenties, I was a bit of a hothead. Lucky for most of us, age tends to mellow our emotions.

"I will see what I can do," was the only response I received.

"Thank you!" I responded, trying to remain calm.

Before first period, several days later, while correcting papers, Jake appeared out of nowhere as he usually did. Looking me straight in the eyes, Jake said, "You called the newspaper didn't you?"

Feeling caught by the gills like a hanging dead salmon in a fish net, I asked, "What are you talking about?"

Jake just looked at me, smiled, and walked away. Not telling a lie, I just did not answer his question.

Jake's heroic actions were just that, heroic. Jake did not want recognition and was happy just knowing that he had done a good deed.

To this day, Jake taught me a valuable lesson; "True heroes do not need recognition."

Hero: Teen-ager's fast action may have saved 2-year-old's life.

BY BRUCE RUSHTON

The News Tribune

Jake Jones found a quick way to make new friends when he ran into the house of a family he didn't know and saved the life of a choking infant.

Jones, 15 was just finishing a water fight at his parent's house across the street when the crisis began.

Upon hearing that the girl was choking, Jake, who says he has never taken a first aid course, hurdled a four-foot fence and ran inside the house.

"She was all purple," recalled Jake of Sabrina's condition. Jones began pounding on the upside-down girls back. Despite hearing tiny gasps, he continued pounding. "I wasn't sure if it was out."

Finally, Sabrina began crying and the crisis was over.

Sandy credits Jake with dislodging the obstruction and saving Sabrina's life.

Sabrina now runs to Jake when he visits the family. On a recent visit, Jake seemed to be the only person who held Sabrina's attention as he cradled her and quieted her screams for a soft drink.

Sandy said that a few days after the incident, a neighbor expressed surprise that Jake would care enough to come over to the aid of someone he didn't know.

Jake, who said he was released from probation last February for offenses including assault and trespassing, acknowledges that he has a less-than-stellar reputation in the eyes of some of his neighbors, but he says he has matured since his last brushes with the law.

Jake recently began playing basketball and other games once a week with a 6-year-old Stanley Elementary School student who suffers from behavior and emotional disorders.

Darrell Hamlin, a teacher at Region V Learning Center, said that despite poor attendance at Stadium High School, Jake is doing well after transferring to the alternative school.

"This is like the last-chance ranch down here," Hamlin said. He added, "I cannot understand why Jake could not be motivated in a regular high school.

"He's a fine example and role model in P.E. (physical education) class," said Hamlin. "Jake is just a great young man. Why can't the regular ed schools keep a kid like that?"

20. Coincidence

As I've already mentioned a few times, it is striking how coincidences involving former Region 5 Learning Center students continued to occur so many years later.

The other day, getting ready to go to the city dump, almost as an afterthought, I called the Tacoma city dump's "call to haul" program to have an old refrigerator picked up and taken to the dump for free.

After receiving my address and full name, the receptionist asked, "Are you a teacher?" After answering, I was pleasantly surprised to learn that the receptionist was Jake Jones's mother and that after all these years she recognized my name.

Listening to her talk, I thought, "Why are these coincidences happening?" Trying to make sense of the developing event, I blurted out, "I have had Jake in my thoughts for weeks, and now I am talking to you, his mother." I was astonished at our chance conversation.

Seeming just as surprised, she mentioned, "Jake was talking about you over the Christmas holidays also."

As we talked about Jake, I mentioned the incident when he'd saved the little neighborhood girl from choking to death on a piece of hot dog caught in her throat. I asked, "Has Jake been in contact with the girl?" Jake's mother indicated that he had not.

I expressed to her, "I think that situation could have been the turning point in Jake's life."

When she did not respond, I told her light-heartedly, "Jake was a bit of a rascal, but he was one of my favorite students."

Grasping for conversation, I went on to mention, "At Ohop Lake, while he was fishing, Jake walked right off the back of the dock." We both laughed.

Jake's mother proudly proclaimed, "Jake expressed to me that he was happy that I was tough on him."

From what I recall, it was evident that Jake's mother had not started being a parent when he was fifteen years old and in trouble. It was obvious that Jake had been held and nurtured a lot as a child. He was mischievous, but his heart glowed with happiness. Most parents that we dealt with at Region 5 were doing catch-up work. Parenting starts at day one—you don't start parenting when kids get into trouble.

Jake's mother referred to it as being "tough." I refer to it as "time spent." People through the years have asked me many times, "What is your secret to working with troubled youth?" I would calmly explain, "Time and listening is the only secret I have. Spending time and listening to kids makes the difference. You can have all the money in the world, but if you do not spend time with your children, they will be a reflection of something or someone else."

Jake was a reflection of his mother and was a great kid, who from the sounds of it, grew into a fine man.

Jake's mother thanked me several times for the work that I had done for him. I told her, "Jake was easy." I could tell from her voice that she was very proud of him and what he had accomplished since attending Region 5. I do not know how much we helped Jake, but he had come back from the dark side to become a productive citizen.

Sharing his phone number, she paused, "He would love to talk to you." Following that comment, I gave her my phone number and my appreciation.

As we ended our conversation, she urged, "Jake would love to hear from you."

Hanging up, with Jake's number in hand, an apprehensive feeling began growing in my conscience, "Should I make the call or not?"

21. Social Shadows

everal months later, I finally got up the courage to call Jake. When Jake answered the phone, I tried to identify the voice to the memories. Recognizing his voice, I could tell that age and experience were etched into it. After introducing myself, nervously, I repeated my first and last name several times.

Disappointed, it took several seconds for Jake to recall who I was. For some reason I did not mention Region 5 Learning Center as reference for recognition. Feeling the vibrations of his brain through to my home phone, I imagined his memories moving rapidly to visualize some of the adventures that we had taken together.

"I recognized your voice right off. You are one of the most fun students that I've ever worked with," I said, breaking the silence. "It was weird to call the city dump and come in contact with your mom."

"Yeah, Mom told me that she talked to you."

Jake began describing his family and sounded confident in his conversation. "I am living in the Truman Lake area, married, and have three children."

"I have two kids myself," I hesitantly slipped in.

In what seemed like an afterthought he added, "Two are twins, and we have an older daughter."

Interesting, I recall thinking that he said "we", not I.

"What fun that must be," I said, which was followed by more silence.

Again breaking the silence, I started talking about the incident regarding saving the little girl's life during his water balloon fight. Jake was surprised to learn that I was the one who'd contacted *The News Tribune*. Pausing, he said, "I didn't know how *The News Tribune* found out."

I proudly explained to him, "I had to bum rush *The News Tribune* staff to get them to respond."

Laughed, as monumental an event as it was, Jake did not extend the conversation for self glory.

As if an event popped into Jake's mind, he said, "That was nice that you took the time to do all the trips with us."

We exchanged memories of him walking off the dock, holding Bigfoot's private parts, and I realized that we remembered things differently. It was interesting listening to him and realizing that our memories retained certain events and left out others. We were intricately fitting pieces of a puzzle together without knowing. It was weird talking to Jake, now in his thirties and yet visualizing him being fifteen. It was like watching old childhood 30mm movies for the first time in fifteen years.

Listening to Jake, it made me realize that people remember past events differently and not always accurately. Jake's flashback as a fifteen-year-old festive kid and matching them to a twenty-five-year-old who was now fifty-one was eerie.

Toward the end of our conversation, Jake explained several times, "Region 5 was not where I should have been."

With no disrespect intended, I said, "I am sure that most of the students that attended Region 5 felt that they did not deserve to be there either."

As if caught in thought, Jake did not respond to my reply.

I do not remember why Jake was at Region 5 and it doesn't matter. What matters is that he is a better person as a result of attending there. I am not sure what influence we had upon him, but Region 5 gave Jake time to better prepare for high school.

Most of the students that we had at Region 5 began their life of crime at either age fourteen or fifteen. The high school system of ninth through twelfth grades in the Tacoma school system has failed. Ninth graders are too young for high school. As a result, Tacoma School District has had a current dropout rate of 55 percent, three years in a row.

Jake was adamant when he said, "I do not know why I was sent there." Regardless, we either set him straight or he decided he did not want to be criminal.

To be honest, I was proud to hear that Jake was ashamed to be at Region 5 Learning Center. There is no glory in being a criminal. Region 5 had the reputation of being a gang school of criminals. Most of the Hilltop Crips gang members lived close enough that they could walk to school.

Of course we tried to dispel that negative label, but the truth of the matter was that most of the students attending Region 5 were rough gang court-connected students. Jake was not one of those students.

Mostly to comfort Jake, I said "Your mother made an interesting comment to me when we were talking on the phone. She expressed proudly that you had thanked her for being tough on you."

Pausing, I let my comment sink in and said, "She referred to it as tough love."

Jake did not respond, waiting. I wondered if he was contemplating his own parenting skills.

"Jake, it probably didn't take a lot of tough love to get you back on track." I added, "Your mother started loving you and taking an interest in you from the start."

Jake did not reply.

As our conversation was winding down, I asked, "What was your favorite road trip?" Expecting him to bring up the incident at

Ohop Lake, instead, he said, "The Squim Animal Game farm was my favorite road trip, and I recently took my kids there."

Pausing as if trying to expel the correct words, like a little kid, Jake laughed. "I remember being in the huge orange van scared to death when the buffalo stuck his huge hairy head inside the open sliding door."

Surprised, I added, "I had totally forgotten about that."

We were studying World War II and the potential Japanese invasion after the Pearl Harbor attack on December 7, 1941, so Moressa and I decided to take a road trip to Fort Warden, Washington. We wanted the students to experience our state's coastal defenses against a Japanese invasion.

On the way to Fort Warden we stopped by the Squim Game Farm to see the wild animals. The more dangerous animals were penned up—bears, rhinoceroses, and tigers. What Jake recalled most vividly were the free-roaming animals. Over several hundred acres of land elk, llamas, deer, and bison roamed freely.

Before we entered the free-roaming range, we were given several loaves of bread to feed the animals. Driving in the van through the open-roaming area, we were able to feed the animals through the slightly opened windows. We learned very quickly that llamas will spit in your face as you feed them. By feeding them through a slightly opened window and quickly rolled it up, we avoided the llama's rapid fire saliva.

When we fed the bison, they would brush up right next to the window for their piece of bread. As Jake was reliving the story, I began to recall quite clearly what happened next.

Not remembering who did it, but someone slid open the side door to the van. The closest bison to the open door slipped his huge head inside for a bread snack.

"I have never seen so many tough-guy wanna-be gang members leap to the back seat of the van so quickly," I joked.

Jake, with a laugh, said, "I remember sitting on the front bench seat and all I could see was a huge hairy head with horns."

"Do you remember the nasty smell of the bison's breath?" I asked.

"It was its long green pointed tongue that was sweeping around looking for more bread that stunk," Jake replied laughing.

As we joked back and forth, I got an icky feeling remembering jumping from the driver's bucket seat, passing in front of the huge Bison's head and getting slimed across my arms by its pointed saliva-dripping green tongue.

I asked Jake, "Do you remember how we got the bison's head out of the van?"

"It happened so fast I don't remember."

I went on to recall with him, "With all the tough guys and gangbangers piled in the back seat wetting their pants, grabbing the sliding door handle, I slammed the door into its head three or four times before he pulled out."

As we laughed about the situation, I thought, "Only at Region 5…"

Hearing faint sounds of traffic in the background, I suspected that Jake was on his cell phone while driving when he slowly ended our conversation. Interestingly enough, I have to ask myself, "Why was I hesitant to talk with Jake.

Sadly, more often than not, I read about former students involved in crimes reported by *The News Tribune*. The recent huge "Tacoma Hilltop Crip" gang roundup by state law officials was shocking. More startling was that I recognized almost half of the gangsters' mug shots.

It was reassuring talking to Jake that maybe our efforts at Region 5 were not wasted.

Now more than ever, I wanted to know, "Where are the rest of the social shadows from Region 5 Learning Center?"

22. Mack and Clark

After talking to Jake, one morning, for no apparent reason, another student emerged out of my recessed memories, Clark.

Many years ago, unannounced as usual, Margaret's successor as roving principal of Tacoma School District's alternative education programs, roared in. As with most of his whirlwind visits, everything had to be dropped and we had to meet immediately. Mack, with his rushed and panicked manner, needed us.

Mack was rubbing his bald head and pacing back and forth, so we knew that we had a huge favor to comply with. As usual, he started off, "State law says every student deserves an education."

There was no doubt in any of our minds that Mack believed and lived by the RCW, the Revised Codes of Washington State law. On several occasions he would battle the Tacoma District for alternative education students. He was a warrior for the underdog.

As he rambled, I wondered what was up. What could be so serious that he had to rush over in a panic?

"We have a situation," Mack said with much energy and drama. "No matter what his crime was, he deserves an education. He has been released on bail and is awaiting a retrial for his charges. No other school in the county will touch this one."

Pausing to rub his head, he continued, "I was asked to find a school for this boy and this is the only program that can handle this."

Mack looked everyone, one by one, in the eyes. "The student is Clark from Spanaway."

After another pause, Mack said, "We all know what he did."

Everyone in the state who read the news or watched the television knew what Clark had done. In fact, I am sure that many parents in the area were contemplated locking their bedroom doors at night as a result of the allegations against him.

With an emanating silence enveloping us, bringing us back from the abyss, I said, "Well, I would like to meet Clark before we decide."

Everyone just looked at me as if to say, "What is wrong with you? No way we take this guy!"

After popping off, I recall sinking lower in my seat and thinking, "Why do I always open my mouth?"

Mack let it hang for a minute and fired back before I could recant, "I'll arrange it!" and then left like a passing lightning storm.

The conversation after Mack's drama was simple: how do we deal with this guy?

Accompanied by Arnie Stevens, several days later, Mack, Clark, his father, and grandmother showed up after school for the interview.

Arnie was nick named the "gate keeper." His responsibility was to strategically place students in programs that best meet their needs and more importantly, for the safety of others. Evil was slowly creeping in to our schools like the 14th century Black Death of Europe. Arnie took his responsibilities seriously and as the gate keeper, we trusted his advice more than anyone else in the district. He was a valued team member, if Mack was unavailable; he was the man for advice.

As we sat there, we were trying to sense the flaws, but the Clark's seemed like a normal everyday all-American family.

The room was eerily quiet as we looked over Clark. "This is not the guy that the papers described," I thought. At the time, I would never have connected him with his crime.

Clark resembled the neighborhood boy next door that you would pay to mow your lawn. I even got the feeling that I could trust him with my house keys to take care of our animals while on vacation. He reminded me of a well-educated, clean-cut kid who would never get mixed up with the law.

From the expressions in the room, we were all wondering the same thing: "Who is this guy?" From his appearance, Clark had to be innocent. I recall thinking without saying, "It is no wonder that the jury could not reach a verdict." We were confused; Clark was not at all what we suspected.

Mack explained the particulars and Clark's father made a plea for us to take him, and really, after meeting the guy, there was no reason to refuse the request.

Looking to Arnie for advice, Moressa asked, "What do you think?"

In a matter of fact tone, Arnie said, "This is the best program in Tacoma for this situation." Glancing around the room, he continued, "There is nowhere else for Clark to go, except home bound tutoring."

After the decision was agreed upon, as a group, we did the Region 5 behavioral and dress code contracts that very day. After Clark and his family left, we shared our different interpretations of him. The common theme we considered was, "How will this one turn out?"

Clark's first couples of weeks at Region 5 were uneventful. He was eager to do anything requested of him. If we had asked him to run up the side of a building, he would have tried.

Clark immediately wanted to be in the life sports program, but I told him, "You will have to wait and earn the privilege the same as everyone else." Eventually, with court approval and a perfect behavior performance, Clark earned the privilege of being involved in Region 5's extracurricular activities.

In addition to being in the life sports program, after special permission from the prosecutor's office, Clark was able to go out of town on road trips with the platoon. He was like a caged animal and could not wait to get out of Tacoma.

Before Clark's first road trip, I was a bit apprehensive to have him along. Overly stern, I instructed him, "I am your shadow. You need to stay right with me on the entire road trip." Clark, of course, was compliant. I suspected that he was just happy to be free and in the mountains. Still, before we left Region 5, we searched and researched everyone, and every backpack in the van. We were taking no chances.

For added security, I asked Hugh Thomson our building special education instructor to come along. Hugh was a gentle giant of a man who volunteered for the Vietnam War so that his older brother would not be drafted. During his tours of duty, he was responsible for combat supplies dispatched to secret operations in battles that were off the grid. With his logistics experiences, he could have easily been making huge amounts of money in the private sector; instead, he opted to dedicate himself to helping disadvantaged youth.

During Clark's first road trip with the platoon, the drive to Mount Rainer National Park was uneventful. As usual, stopping at the Alder Lake Dam which is adjacent to the Mountain Highway, I gave my standard lecture about the dam, the Depression, and Franklin Delano Roosevelt's plan to put people back to work.

I recall that everyone was quietly listening when Clark raised his hand and inquired, "Is this one of the dams built by Roosevelt's economic recovery program?"

Surprised, I replied, "Yes."

Clark continued, "Was it designed to put back to work the twenty-five percent of the population that was unemployed during the Depression?"

Everyone, including myself, turned and looked at Clark. After a moment of silence, with the Alder Lake Dam in the background, I simply said, "You are absolutely right." Clark was a smart guy.

Piling back into the van, Clark was left alone by the other students. Some had done time with him in the Pierce County Remann Hall juvenile detention center and had not warmed up to him yet. Looking through the rearview mirror, I noticed that they did not eagerly choose to sit next to him. He was quiet and kept to himself.

Unloading at Longmire, about twenty miles inside the Mount Rainier National Park; our day's hike was called Rampart Ridge. I usually start out the road trip season with several short hikes, one to get in shape and the other to weed out the wimps.

Hiking with young aggressive boys was not easy, and I generally bent the rules letting them hike on their own. It would have been impossible to have them hike in single file; they were not Boy Scouts.

I had only one mandatory request that they had to follow: the "Boy Scout Buddy System." Everyone had to hike with a buddy; if not, I would threaten them by saying, "You will never ride with me again if you break this rule!" With that said, with Hugh in the lead, they were off to explore and enjoy the Pacific Northwest.

I do not remember much about the hike itself. I do remember hiking with Clark, or I should say hiking behind him. Generally, I am not interested in a student's crimes. At age fifteen I got into trouble and was given a clean slate, so I figured that I would give the students at Region 5 the same fresh start. Clark's situation was different and curiosity got the best of me. After following Clark for about a mile, without stopping, without eye contact, I asked, "What happened?"

Clark did not miss a step and never turned around to answer.

Abruptly halting, Clark half turned toward me, but did not look at me. It was a clear day, and when I slightly turned my eyes toward the direction of his gaze, I was also caught in awe. From our vantage point, Mount Rainier appeared close enough to touch.

I vividly recall that when we both stopped to look at the mountain, pausing, without making eye contact, Clark simply replied, "I don't know."

Looking at Clark, I sensed no evil. Some students carry evil on them like a bad smell. Clark did not have a glow about him, but evil was not permeating from his soul.

Having no idea what answer to expect, caught off guard, I did not respond. I am sure that he had been asking himself the same question a thousand times: "What happened?"

After a longer than normal look at the gleaming snow-covered mountain, we turned away in silence and continued our hike.

I never brought it up again.

To this day, believing that Clark did not know why he did it, I still wonder, "How could a nice guy like Clark, do such an evil thing?"

23. Tutor

I n the classroom, academically, Clark was heads above everyone else.

Sometimes I thought that Clark knew more than I did in regard to particular subject areas. Still, he never let on to the other students or the staff just how smart he really was.

It was not hard for other students to figure out that Clark was intelligent. Clark had probably learned from his time locked up in Remann Hall that revenge was the common mode of dealing with damaged egos. As smart as he was, he never belittled anyone for his or her lack of knowledge. I am sure that Clark learned at an early age that there were many ways to belittle a person without saying a word. Watching Clark, I noticed that he had become street smart enough to know that if he "punked" some of the guys at Region 5, they would get him later.

After a few weeks of class, I noticed Clark was continuing to finish his assignments early. One day, pretending to be too busy to answer a question from a student, not looking up, I said, "Clark, can you help him out?"

Not making eye contact with either of them, making the request, I kept busy with my make-believe work.

That is how it started—Clark became the class tutor.

Surprisingly, students were very receptive to Clark's assistance. He had a charm about him that said, "I am just a nice guy trying to help out." Students with low self-esteem and huge gaps in their acquisition of knowledge can smell out arrogance in a heartbeat. Clark had a calm way of putting lower-performing students at ease.

Clark was an excellent peer tutor.

24. Hollow Brown Eyes

On another occasion that I recall, Clark gave me a scary feeling.

While at the Boys and Girls Club, Clark, with about twenty minutes left before we had to head back to Region 5, challenged me to a one-on-one basketball match. I thought to myself, "Why not? Neither one of us can jump."

The game was all in good fun and Clark had a bit of a lead when I thought, "This guy is an athlete too?"

I was almost ready to let Clark win when he made an offhand comment under his breath. At first I wasn't sure what he'd said, so I asked him to repeat it.

In a mocking tone Clark said, "You're getting too old to keep up."

"What?" I said, caught by surprise. I rarely ever heard a negative comment from Clark. "Is that so," I muffled out.

The next several minutes were a battle, man on man, and we had major honor at stake. Both of us were bumping, throwing elbows, and jamming each other for the win. It was an intense match, and if I was going to get beat, it was not going to be a result of my age.

Huffing and puffing, we were both tired when I caught a spooky glare from Clark.

Checking the ball with him at the free throw line after taking the lead back, I caught a peep into Clark's eyes. Focusing on the ball, not making eye contact, he just mechanically gave me the ball.

Peered in, I saw deep hollow brown eyes. Clark's eyes were scary to the point that I thought, "Maybe I should let him win." It was the deep vacant hollow look that was frightening. His eyes were vacant to the point that I thought about calling the game off and saving "face" for the both of us.

There were many occasions during life sports competitions that halfway through an intense volleyball or basketball match, as a result of growing tensions, I would bring an abrupt halt to the activity. This was one of those tense moments, but since it was only Clark and I competing, we continued the match.

After the match, Clark did not take the one-on-one basketball competition well. He deescalated quickly, but was not happy.

Reflecting back, I often wonder whether I had witnessed some of Clark's hidden rage that day. For him to commit the crime that he was accused of, his rage was deep and well hidden.

I did win the match.

25. Lake George

I t was probably November or it could have been October, I am not really sure. In regard to the year in "man time," say ten to fifteen years ago. As with most males, recalling events by year and dates is difficult. I recall visual events.

Not remembering the month or year, I took the platoon on a ten-mile hike on the West Side Road of Mount Rainier National Park. Our destination was an alpine lake named Lake George.

Twice a year I would take the platoon to Lake George, on this particular day we had four staff members and about fourteen students. Some of the probation and parole officers wanted to join us. As a result, we had Region 5 students who had not been hiking with us before.

After parking the van and distributing the hiking gear, I reviewed trail etiquette and safety procedures. I was most adamant about not cutting the trail switchbacks. Glancing at a group of Hilltop Crip gang members, I could tell by the look in their eyes that they had no idea what I was talking about.

"Look, the trail will cut back and forth," I explained. "Have you ever ridden your bike up a steep hill and cut back and forth to try and peddle up the hill without stopping?"

"No, but I let the emergency brake off and watched a car roll down a hill," one of the Crips said with a snicker looking around for reinforcement. I felt proud that the only students who laughed were those who had not earned their platoon membership status.

Locking eyes, without saying a word, and winning the stare-down with the Crip, I continued, "You never cut through the switchbacks. If you get off trail, you could get lost."

Reviewing the safety instructions again for reinforcement, I noticed that Clark was sitting next to Smiley again. "Weird the shortest and skinniest student at Region 5 was good buddies with Clark," keeping my thoughts to myself.

Smiley was his nickname. I can picture his face, but I cannot remember his name. Remember that he was always smiling; I think he was a burglar. As small as he was he would have no trouble squeezing through narrow entries of unsuspecting homes and businesses.

Reflecting back, I did overhear Smiley one day bragging about breaking into a house through a skylight. As he was telling the story, I recall thinking, "What a sneaky guy."

Weird how memories resurface, I recall a sad conversation with Smiley's P.O. several years after our hike to Lake George when Smiley had moved on. One afternoon, I happened to ask Arthur, "How is Smiley doing?"

Arthur explained, "Smiley ended up in Walla Walla State Prison."

I was surprised. No way would Smiley have committed rape or murder. Walla Walla was a tough place, and Smiley was not a tough guy.

Arthur went on to tell me that he was headed over to see him that week.

"Wow, that's a long way to drive from Tacoma to Walla Walla," I said.

Arthur who was retired ex-military gave me an unexpected sorrowful look and said, "He got caught by the wolf pack."

Having no immediate response, I tried not to visualize little Smiley getting caught by the prison's wolf pack and used. At the time, as I am now recalling our conversation, I feel sick to my stomach. Smiley was an excellent platoon member, and I would have almost trusted him with my wallet.

Still in shock, I asked Arthur, "What happened?"

Arthur went on to explain, "He burglarized the neighborhood sheriff's house and stole some guns. He was at Walla Walla with no money and someone offered to loan him some smokes."

Arthur, pausing and shaking his head slowly continued, "He did not have cigarettes or the money to repay the debt."

Arthur again paused, taking a breath and holding back his emotions said, "They sold him to the highest bidders."

After all the good times we'd shared, I could not bring myself to visualize such an evil demoralizing event. "Animals!" I said with disgust.

Without making eye contact, Arthur mumbled out, "He had to have reconstruction, and he will be in the prison infirmary for some time."

Usually I ask the probation officers to tell their clients hello. Not this time. No way did I ever want Smiley to know that I was aware of what had been done to him. I was speechless and very sad. I hoped that as a result of such a vicious attack, that Smiley would never join the prison's wolf pack and victimize other naive prisoners.

Trying to grasp the horror of Smiley's future challenges and reflecting back on the day that we hiked to Lake George, I was glad that we had given Smiley some good memories to ponder upon during his recovery.

Getting back to the hike to Lake George, one of the most bewildered hikers was McFly. He was a new student, and I probably would not have taken him on the hike except that his parole officer made the request. Robert Smalls was his P.O. and a strong supporter of the Region 5 life sports activities.

Robert Smalls was from the South and had escaped from there via the military. He did his twenty-plus years in the service of his country and retired. Similar to several of the parole officers of the Washington State Juvenile Rehabilitation Administration, he used his military experience to become an excellent parole officer.

Smalls was a stocky five foot eight, all smiles and fun. But, if his clients thought that he was a pushover, they were dead wrong. It was assumed that he must have been a drill sergeant at one time; when he gave a student a dressing down, the entire building could hear it. Even behind closed doors, down the hall, Smalls could be heard. He was a gentle man, but at the same time, he was no one to mess with.

For further backup, Hugh was along for the hike. Being a natural with the students, Hugh had a perpetual smile that was inviting to everyone. In tense situations, he could put everyone at ease.

As usual, the new students had no idea what they were getting themselves into. We had to hike about four miles to the Lake George trailhead and hike another mile into the lake. It was no easy task.

It was in the 1940s or maybe the 1950s that the Mount Rainier National Park had a huge mudslide washing away the access bridge to the once well-maintained Westside Road. For some reason, the National Park Service did not repair the road or the bridge that was washed out. As a result, we had to use large river boulders to cross the tributary river that eventually fed into the Nisqually River. Once across the river, the first four miles were on an uphill unused and over-grown grassy gravel road.

During the hike, the steep switchbacks along the overgrown gravel road were physically taxing for the inexperienced hikers. We were continually yelling at them not to cut through the switchbacks. The new hikers were constantly trying to sneak a shortcut. I remember reminding them, "There are no shortcuts in life and no shortcuts in the platoon!" The worst switchback-cutters were the Crips from the Hilltop.

Knowing it would be easy to miss the Lake George trailhead and end up hiking the Westside Road for another four miles to a dead end. About three miles into the hike, leaving the slower hikers who were in the middle of the pack with Smalls, I asked Hugh to bring up the rear of the platoon.

Catching Clark, Smiley, and a few other members of the platoon before they overshot the trailhead was no easy task. Walking and running, by the time I caught them I was out of breath.

Gathering the group, I noticed that Clark had emerged as the leader. I sensed without asking that he and his father must have been hikers. He conveyed confidence and leadership. Smiley, on the other hand, appeared disorientated and had no trail experience. Lucky for him he was a quick learner.

As we were waiting to hit the last mile of the hike, with time to spare before the rest of the students joined us, Clark and Smiley were scouting out the area. Not too far from the Lake George trailhead they discovered a hidden raised rock platform. Mirrored by the forest, they stumbled across a aging forgotten monument.

At first glance it did not appear to be anything of importance. It was a platform of raised rocks that had gotten overgrown with grass and saplings. The neglected patch of rocks and grass were stationed to the right side of the road. Surprisingly, as many trips to Lake George as we had made, no one had ever noticed it before.

As we gathered silently and read the words on the oxidized plaque, it turned out to be a World War II War memorial. Glancing up toward the South Tahoma Glacier on Mount Rainier, I recall being lost in thought. Bringing me back, Clark was the first to finish reading and quietly commented, "What a sad event."

Finishing scanning the thirty-two dead marines' names, I looked again through the gap in the trees and pointed. "That has to be where these poor guys crashed. Why else would all the trees be gone in the direction of the Tahoma glacier?"

As more of the platoon members staggered into the area with Smalls, we motioned them over to the forgotten memorial. The rock staging on which the memorial was posted was large enough for all of us to stand. Once there, I requested that every student read the marine memorial then sit and wait for everyone else to join.

Last but not least, Hugh brought with him the last of the stragglers.

Standing quietly next to Hugh as he read the plaque, I noticed that his perpetual smile had dissipated. Sharing the same thoughts without saying a word, we locked eyes, turned, looked at our bunch of undisciplined outlaws and just shook our heads.

Being a teacher, there was no way that I was going to miss this learning opportunity. With this large of a group and some of the new students who had not been on road trips with the platoon before, it was hard for me to get their attention. From out of nowhere, with much emotion, Smalls in his drill sergeant voice bellowed out, "Quiet!"

Everyone went still. Besides hearing his commanding voice echo through the forest, the only thing we could hear was our own breathing.

Breaking the silence and knowing that Clark was probably the best reader in the group, I asked him to read the memorial out loud. With Smalls and Hugh on guard, every student listened in silence and developed a personal interpretation of the tragic event.

After Clark was done, I explained the short version of the situation to the group. "In 1946, before Christmas, a group of thirty-two marines were flying home from San Francisco and crashed into Mount Rainier."

Letting it hang for a moment, I went on to explain, "Surviving World War II, these poor guys unexpectedly crashed into a mountain!"

Glancing around at the group sitting quietly, I thought to myself, "They don't get it." I could tell that Smalls and Hugh, being military men got it and were a bit emotional.

Looking at the group I yelled, "You guys don't get it, do you?" Pausing, I blurted out, "These guys survived the most deadly event thrust upon mankind!"

I went on, "They witnessed mankind's worst chapter in world history!"

Pausing to deal with the sadness, I felt horrible for the dead marines encased in the glacier. Looking around at the lack of empathy, I began to pity the members of the group that had no idea what I was talking about. I continued, "Do you get it? These poor souls survive the war, were expecting to have the holidays with their families, and crashed into the South Tahoma Glacier."

Glancing around, I noticed that the group was silent and watching my every move. "These brave soldiers had everything to live for, and now they are dead and forgotten."

As I scanned the group, the silence was eerie. Eying the glacier I said, "Think about your life, the mistakes you have made. You have a choice. These guys had no choice. Look up there. That's where they are to this day!"

I let the moment hang. "You can choose your future." I could feel the quiet of the mountains encompassing the group as they tried to perceive the unexpected events that had unfolded in 1946.

Easing the tension, Smalls, Hugh and I made each platoon member glance at the list of thirty-two dead World War II marines who had crashed on Mount Rainier.

"Encased in a glacier covered with snow on Mount Rainier," I repeated one more time before we left the memorial.

I would like to think that most of the hikers that day got the message about personal choice. Most of the veteran platoon members appeared to understand what I was talking about. Most Region 5 students had done time in the confinement of Washington's juvenile prisons. The students who had experienced being locked away from their families seemed to have a more worldly perspective on events like this. Maybe it was a loss of their freedom that made the difference.

Making brief eye contact with Clark, I sensed that he got the message—life and death, what control do we really have?

Meandering away from the memorial like a herd of elk wandering across a highway, for no apparent reason, I silently pondered, "Which one of these guys will be the next unexpected death?"

Heading for the trailhead that was nestled into the evergreen forest, unlike the slightly overgrown Westside Road, we hit deep snow. As a reflex and not a thought, before we entered the trail, I gave a request to Clark and Smiley. "You're responsible for leading the group into Lake George." My instructions were specific. "Do not go out onto the lake if it is frozen."

As we entered the trail, we were lucky; it had been a while since it had snowed and left behind from previous hikers was a continual path of footstep indentations in the snow for us to follow. Smalls took the rear to make sure no one turned back, Hugh was with the lead group and I was the floater roaming along the trail issuing confidence and encouragement.

On the trail, pausing, from a distance, I noticed skinny McFly breaking the rules and hiking alone. Maybe it was confidence or maybe no one else wanted to be near him, I do not recall. As McFly got closer, noticing that his sweatshirt was soaking wet, I recall feeling a chill just looking at him. I did not know McFly, but I did learn he had great courage. Hiking with no coat, a crooked baseball cap, and without gloves, he was an example of a brave, but lost "soul." The only thing keeping him warm was a wet sweatshirt. It was a pitiful sight of bravery, but one to admire.

Continuing to watch, I recall thinking, "What a weird guy." McFly had a quirky body movement about him. His frail body moved in a jerky sort of way. His wet blond curly hair hanging out around his baseball cap was in a messy tangle. He had the crooked smile of a stroke victim that begged for help. Feel a little pity for him, I thought, "What is his story?"

Watching every quirky step that he took, McFly did not know that I was watching him until he was almost right in front of me.

"Are you cold?" I asked.

Out of his purple crooked lips he responded, "Are you?"

"Good question," I sheepishly responded, wearing shorts and giving my hat and gloves to another unprepared student.

After a pause, I said, "Yes, but not as cold as you look."

McFly appeared to be on a quest, and I could tell by the look on his face that nothing was going to deter him.

"Hold on for a minute," I shot out. "We need to warm you up." Looking at his feet, noticing that he did not have any socks on, I asked, "Where are your socks?"

Without time for a response, I further inquired, "Did you get the list of hiking supplies that I requested you bring along?"

Bypassing my question, without making eye contact, McFly said, "I have never done anything like this before."

As Smalls and four Hilltop Crips appeared on the scene, I explained to them, "McFly is in a tough situation, and we have to help him out."

Ignoring me, the Crips almost walked right by me as if I were not there. Moving into their path, I explained, "Look! We need to help this guy out!"

It was a standoff. Four and a half miles into the Cascade Mountains and there was no going through me. I could tell that when they looked at McFly, they were thinking, "Help this crazy white guy, no way!"

Maintaining eye contact, I said with emphasis, "We are the North Star Platoon up here. We need to stick together." I was stern, not commanding in my request. We were at a stalemate with neither side giving an inch.

Breaking the deafening silence, Smalls was the first to act. Whipping off his backpack, Smalls ordered McFly, "Sit here and take off your shoes!"

Distracting us from our power struggle, we all shared a look of disbelief. McFly, not knowing what was going to happen next, quickly complied with the order. After sitting down, Smalls took off his coat and stuck McFly's feet into his armpits. I could tell by the look on their faces that the Crips were stunned. "What the heck?" is all I recall thinking.

"Okay, fellas. What do you have to help out?" I hastily mumbled out.

"I got extra socks," one of the stunned blue guys said.

From one of the other blue guys: "I got a shirt if he needs it."

With McFly's feet warming up in Small's armpits, we all threw in what we had to help out. From my backpack I gave McFly one of my dry shirts.

After a few minutes, McFly's shaking subsided and his lips started to regain their natural appearance. Once McFly's feet were warmer and he had some dryer clothes on, I quietly suggested to Smalls, "He needs to go back. I don't think he can make it."

"No!" said McFly in his tough guy voice.

Turning and staring, we were all caught off guard by his boldness.

After a moment of thought and looking at the most determined member of the platoon, I said, "Then let's go."

After hiking about another half mile, we crested a snow-covered hill. Standing on the hill I proclaimed like an early explorer, "There it is, Lake George!" Then a thought hit me like a snowball in the face. "I hope no one went out onto the ice."

Putting on the quickstep, I hustled down to the lake before the rest of our group to investigate.

"No one here," I whispered to myself. "Where are they?"

"Look, listen, and think," I told myself as Smalls, McFly, and the Crips grouped up. We were all wondering the same thing without saying a word. "Where did they go?"

"Listen!" I said.

Hearing some laughing off to the left of the frozen lake, we headed in that direction. Moving through the brush that was surrounding the lake and over a slight hill we found the rest of the platoon happily eating their lunches and relaxing. They were happily hunkered down near some aging log structures. It was a relief to see them all together and dry.

"How did you guys get over here?" I asked.

"We followed Clark," Smiley said with pride.

At the time, I wondered, "Is Clark smart enough to manipulate the group away from the tempting ice-covered lake before anyone had the idea to test the ice?"

I will never know.

"Do you guys know who built these log structures?" I asked in my teacher voice.

From somewhere in the group came a response, "Clark told us all about it."

I added, "Then you know that if we were here during the Great Depression, you guys would have been building these log structures rather than feeding your faces under them."

I also reinforced to the new platoon members in particular, "We never leave a trace of evidence to show that we were ever here." In addition, I gave a brief directive regarding the safety etiquette of ice, "Never go on frozen ice!"

Observing Smalls again warming up McFly's feet in his armpits, I remembered to ask for some socks and another dry shirt for McFly. Several platoon members kicked in. Hugh taking over operations helping McFly acquire dry cloths. I was proud to see the group working together.

We were lucky, as we were eating, the sun squeaked out of the clouds to create a cold, but beautiful clear Pacific Northwest day.

As we prepared to hit the one-mile hike out of the woods and the remaining four miles down the West Side Road, I suggested to the platoon that we pick up litter along the way. In my stern fatherly tone, I stated quite clearly, "Do not cut the switchbacks on the road trying to take a shortcut!"

As the platoon headed out, I noticed some litter left behind and asked Smalls and Hugh to lead the group out while I policed up the camp site. To my surprise, without being asked, Clark and Smiley began helping me double check the area. I was impressed.

Once the area was cleaner than we found it, we started heading around the lake to the well-worn snow trail that would lead us out. As we were walking, Clark abruptly stopped appearing mesmerized by the frozen lake.

Smiley, who was always ready to try anything new said, "Let's see how far out on the ice we can go."

Chiding them, I said, "Frozen or not, you know what they did to the only man who walked on water don't you?"

Not getting my joke, Clark and Smiley did not respond.

Gazing out over frozen Lake George, Clark passively commented, "I have never walked on a frozen lake before."

"You won't today either!" I snapped back in a harsher tone than intended. As if not hearing a single word, appearing hypnotized, Clark did not turn away from the frozen lake.

Pausing, lost in thought, for some reason, I remember pondering the fact that given Clark's crime, he may never again get the chance to walk on an ice covered lake.

As we were quietly gazing out at the luring ice covered lake, following the same trail that had brought us in, two hikers approached us from behind. Feeling bad for snapping at Clark, I said, "I have an idea. Let's get a picture of us on the lake." "Break the rules?" Clark said, turning toward me with a sly grin.

After the hikers reached us, we asked them if they would snap a photo of us on the ice. Disregarding their concerns, they were more than happy to comply.

As we lightly stepped out onto the frozen lake, too late, I questioned my decision. The sun had rotated through the sky enough to warm the area, and I was uncertain of how thick the ice really was. Unfortunately, I had learned, once you tell teenagers they can do something, it is almost impossible to turn them back.

Apprehensively, I warned Clark and Smiley, "If you hear a loud whipping sound from the ice, you had better run like mad to the shore!"

It turned out to be an excellent photo of the three of us slightly bending the rules.

In addition to the school photo poster board and the double photos given to individual platoon members, I enlarged two 8×10 photos for Clark and Smiley.

The 8×10 enlargements were of three proud "rule-breakers" posted up on the ice-covered Lake George.

26. Common Sense

The hike back to the van from Lake George was much easier—downhill hiking usually is. In addition, we were in no hurry. I had forgotten to tell the new platoon members that anyone I tagged on the way down the trail would not get a hot fudge sundae. As a result, in no rush, Clark, Smiley, and I walked and ran until we collected as many of the scattered platoon members as we could before we got to the van.

Once at the van, keeping mental track of the platoon members and knowing no one was behind us, I asked, "Where are the blue guys?"

Looking around, Smalls said, "I thought they were with you."

Sensing danger, Hugh responded, "I policed up everyone in front of me".

"No, they are not behind us. I mopped everyone up on the way down," I said, looking back up the overgrown park service road.

"Okay, did anyone see where the blue guys went?" I asked.

Someone answered, "I last saw them cutting the switchbacks."

Worried, shrugging my shoulders, I said to Smalls, "We just have to wait and see."

After about thirty minutes of tense anticipation, I had to take some action. I had to make a decision to find the blue guys ourselves or within an hour to call for search and rescue for help.

Not our friend, darkness was descending on us quickly. Concern was emanating from the group like a ghostly cloud.

In addition to the impending darkness creeping upon us, Smalls also brought to my attention that we had another problem. Several of the guys were on home ankle monitors as part of their early release and had to be home at a certain time.

Looking back up the road, I did not respond. "What else?" I recall thinking.

"Okay, I hate to do this, but we have to split the platoon. Who needs to go home?" I asked.

Looking at Hugh, grasping, I thought, "He has to be the one."

Making eye contact, without speaking a word between us, Hugh said, "Don't worry, I got it."

As three fourths of the platoon left with Hugh and the other probation officers, time was running out. If the sun set with the blue guys lost in the woods, I was done. All I could hear were Margaret's words in the back of my mind, "If you break the law, you're on your own." I am sure Margaret's successor Mack would also have hung me out to dry.

"We can't wait any longer," I fired out. Looking at Smalls, I said, "I am going to run up the trail to the switchbacks to see if I can find where they went off trail. If I cannot find them by the time I get back, we have to notify search and rescue."

Smalls and I both knew what that meant—we were dead meat. Reflecting back on the situation, I have to admire Smalls for sticking it out with me. He could have left me hanging. Instead, he was willing to take the heat with me. He showed great honor.

Before taking off running up the West Side Road, I asked for volunteers. To my surprise McFly jumped to his feet and was the first to verbally volunteer. Rising to stand next to McFly, Clark and Smiley were in, too.

Sizing up McFly's tattered condition and admiring his courage, I did not think he could handle an additional four-mile run, he was wiped out. Sensing his desire and to help him save face, I asked, "Can you stay behind in case Robert needs some help?"

McFly just nodded and admirably looked toward Smalls.

Our running pace, not jogging, was a race against time. Personally, I was wondering what my next career would be if I had to call in search and rescue teams. As weird thoughts were passing through my mind, I regrettably contemplated, "I could go back into roofing houses if I had to."

Running several miles back up the trail, we checked two or three switchbacks with no sign of disturbed plant life to indicate where they cut in. We could not figure out where the blue guys could have gotten off trail. It was as if the forest had swallowed them up; there were no clues left behind.

With no ideas or bodies, we came to the conclusion that they were lost. To be honest, how could a group of 23rd Street Hilltop Crips survive lost in the Cascade Mountains? It was demoralizing to have to head back to the remaining platoon members who were waiting at the van.

We had failed.

About a half a mile or so from the van, I could faintly hear Smalls' roaring voice marching toward us. It must have been the former drill sergeant that emerged. The echo from his voice could probably have been heard for miles afar. The reality was, our careers were safe. The blue guys had somehow made it to the van.

As we got to the van Smalls was just finishing a firm military dressing down of the blue guys. I was just happy that they were not lost or dead.

Out of breath and hiding my relief to see them, I asked, "What happened?" As the shadow of darkness was creeping up on us I just had to know. "Where were you guys?"

"We got off the trail," one of the blue guys said.

Cutting him off, I shouted, "That's why I told you to never leave the trail!" I had to check my anger or I would never hear the entire story.

"We were lost," said another blue guy, almost in panic.

A different blue guy speaking with pride added, "I remembered that you parked by a river."

Now they had my speechless attention, "And?"

"Well, we knew that we didn't cross a river, so we figured we could just follow the river to the van."

Calming down, taking a closer look at the lost blue guys, I could tell by their expressions that they were a bit raddled. I also noticed that their feet and half of their pant legs were soaking wet. Several had cuts and scratches on their faces and arms that were slightly bleeding.

"You will never leave the trail again, will you?"

Ready to continue the lesson, I recall suddenly being distracted by the sounds of the roaring Nisqually River. It was like a voice saying, "You have said enough."

Pausing and gazing out over the river, I could feel my anger diminishing and my heart rate decreasing. I let it go. With everyone safe, the lesson was over.

Without saying a word, I turned from the calming music of the river toward the van. As if by instinct, everyone followed quietly loading in for the journey home.

On the road, before we got to Elbe, the remaining platoon members were fast asleep. Smalls and I were the only two awake in the van.

"We were very lucky today," I said to Smalls with a smile.

Smalls just glanced over at me with the look of an Army veteran. "This was nothin."

27. Survival

Reflecting back upon the Lake George experience, it is remarkable that four Hilltop Crips with no hiking experience were able to calmly work together and save each other.

Roman and I once did a comparison of the Eastside Bloods and the Hilltop Crips to figure out which group had more Special Education labels attached to them.

Researching student files, we discovered that most of the Hilltop Crips (HTC's) were labeled Special Education Severely Behavior Disorder, SBD. That was no surprise to us. The HTC's had more disciplinary suspensions than any other demographic group at Region 5.

In general, the red guys that attended Region 5 tried to stay out of trouble and not attract attention to themselves. Staying "under the radar" made financial sense. The Bloods wanted to be free of the court system to sell drugs.

The HTC's on the other hand, were more often seeking negative attention.

Over the years, I have developed my own special education label for this type of severely behavior disordered student. I call it "L.O.D." or lack of discipline.

Regardless of their labels, the Hilltop Crips taught me a valuable lesson. They were more intelligent than they presented themselves to be. Experienced hikers have gotten lost and have been found naked dead in the woods.

Lost hikers have been known to panic and hike across highways with no idea where they were. Here, we had street kids who had never been to the Mount Rainier National Park, let alone on a ten-mile hike, save themselves.

To this day, I am still amazed at the intelligence and teamwork it took to fight through the woods with no trail to follow and end up at the van.

What genius it was to recall that we parked by a river and then to have the common sense to follow the river to our starting point.

The long-lasting question is, did this experience change their perceptions of their life?

The design of the Region 5 life sports program was to expose inner-city kids to a different lifestyle. We were hoping that by taking crime-impacted students to free parks, the zoo, Northwest Trek, museums, and on exploration hikes that they in turn, rather than committing crimes, would have other positive options.

The million-dollar question we face is, how do we break the criminal cycle?

I believe that to do so, we must expose kids at risk to high-impact positive activities if we expect them to change.

The nice thing about being a human, we can change our behaviors, by changing our thoughts.

Did our plan work; time will tell.

We were blessed that day at the river's edge of the Lake George trailhead and again our Guardian Angels were looking over us. There is no doubt in my mind that if I had lost those Hilltop Crips, no matter what the excuse, I would have been done as a teacher at Region 5.

Did I take some risks?

Yes I did.

Was it worth it?

One day, I will track some of these students down and find out.

28. Gardens

After twenty-three years of teaching court-connected students, I do not know why certain students reemerge in my memory, but McFly is one of them.

After the hike to Lake George, given the continued determination that McFly showed in life sports, I decided to get to know him better. Even with his quirky mannerisms, wild blond curly hair and stroke-victim smile, he was a likable guy.

McFly is an example of the type of student that we spent most of my time at Region 5 protecting. He seemed fragile and was an easy target for bullies.

It is weird, but some fragile weaker students set themselves up as victims for the attention. McFly was not that way—he just did not have any fight left in him. He was like an abused animal walking around, head lowered with his tail between his legs.

I do not understand bullying, but I know that bullies can detect this type victim from miles away.

During my career working with court-connected students, once I became aware of a bully, I watched his or her every move, male or female. My objective was to confront the bullying behaviors and change them. I refer to bullying behaviors as the "big man" syndrome. Most of the large male students that we had at Region 5 were used to yelling and intimidating people to get their way. As a result, they did not develop negotiation skills. By watching their every move, I would document the bullying behaviors and give suggestions on how to better communicate their needs.

If that did not work, I would simply suspend the bully and have a meeting with his or her parole or probation officer.

One day in class, I overheard several students making fun of McFly. They were belittling him for trading favors for cigarettes while he was at the juvenile prison Maple Lane.

I hate bullies and ranking, I was on these guys like a bad smell letting them know that no matter what McFly had done, it would not be brought up at Region 5. Of course, I did threaten to call their probation officers and suspend them just to get their attention.

After the bullies belittled McFly to build their own self-esteem, I could tell by his body language that he was humiliated and embarrassed.

I never asked McFly about Maple Lane and to be honest, it was none of my business. Prison, whether juvenile or adult, is an evil jungle. Whatever McFly had done at Maple Lane, most likely he did it to survive. I have never been in prison, and have no idea what it would be like to be caged up with evil people who act worse than animals.

After McFly had been bullied, I made it a point to look after him. He needed it.

Out of curiosity, I learned that after being released from Maple Lane, McFly was placed in a group home. Being placed in a group home generally indicated to me that a student's home life must be unstable.

In addition, I learned that McFly had a twin sister.

Asking McFly's P.O., Robert Smalls, for more background, I was told that when they were young, McFly and his twin sister were sold by their parents. I was utterly sick when Smalls told me the story. Even after all these years, I still get a sick feeling when thinking about parents selling their children.

From what Smalls told me, being young made the twins a hot commodity on the streets. With that background, it was no wonder that McFly had such weird behaviors.

To this day, it is still startling remembering some of the horrible stories that I have heard regarding what some lowlife scumbag parents have done to their children. It makes me angry that some people are so simple in the head that they would abuse their children.

I never asked McFly about his parents, but now I understand the possibility that he would trade favors for cigarettes. Most likely, he learned at an early age that these types of acts were acceptable. And obviously, McFly learned from his lowlife scumbag parents, that these acts earned rewards.

With all of these factors in mind, when McFly ran from Region 5, he is the only student in my twenty-three-year career that I ever chased down and brought back to school.

Often times when a student had warrants for their arrest or their probation officer was on their way to see them for violations, they would attempt to run out the back door.

Early in my teaching career, I made it a point to never chase students or lay hands on them. I learned early that a simple pat on the shoulder could lead to a physical altercation. Most of the students who attended Region 5 had been abused physically or sexually. From the behaviors that they exhibited, most of our students were also verbally abused at one time or another.

For some reason, and I do not recall what the trouble in question was—McFly had attracted attention to himself at the group home. We had received a call from Smalls that he was coming down to get him. Smalls gave no indication that McFly was going to be arrested. But, somehow our simple-minded Para- educator at the time gave McFly the impression that he was going to be locked up.

Hearing the misinformation, McFly jumped out of his seat and attempted to leave Roman's class.

Trying to contain McFly, Roman was momentarily distracted by another student also jumping out of his seat. As McFly slithered out of Roman's grasp and dashed out, the other student, for unknown reasons, followed in hot pursuit.

Sprinting down the hall, they grabbing the corner of the wall for momentum, and like a jail break took a left turn and dashed out the front door.

As I heard Roman's wingtip dress shoes slapping down the hall, charging by my classroom, he yelled, "McFly is on the run!"

For some reason, Roman showed little concern for the other student, Roman, as I did, felt sorry for McFly.

Jumping out from behind my desk and sprinting toward the action that was unfolding, I heard Roman exit through the Region 5 security door after them.

Not far behind, slamming through the door, side-stepping, I almost knocked Roman off his feet.

Looking left, I could see the two rascals about a half block away from us. Surprisingly, they were walking at a leisurely pace. We knew that if McFly went on the run, once caught, he would be sent directly back to Maple Lane. Knowing his background, taking a chance, I barked at Roman, "You get the other guy, and I'll get McFly."

Being a distance runner in high school and college, I was quite confident that I could run McFly down.

"Hey, McFly, hold up there!" I shouted out.

Once we started after them, they looked back and without speaking a word to each other, darted in different directions.

McFly was crafty. Straining to look over his shoulder, he turned left on South 18th Street and started running up the hill.

Running up the street in an awkward motion, he turned right and headed straight toward several backyards.

Gaining on him, I remember thinking as I entered the first backyard, "I hope no one thinks I'm a burglar and shoots me."

At the time, the Hilltop area of Tacoma was not a friendly location to be running through people's backyards.

Passing through the second yard, I watched McFly jump a fence and hit the ground, running off a roll just like a pro. It was obvious that he had been on the run before.

With ease, I jumped the fence like a steeplechase hurdler to close the gap.

The third and final yard that we ran through had a well-cared-for garden. I remember thinking, "What's a nice garden doing in a place like this?"

Trying to maintain concentration while admiring the stocks of corn, I reached out and snatched up McFly. Not knowing what to expect, grabbing him in a bear hug from behind, I held him tightly.

As time regained its normal speed, with McFly well contained in my bear-hug hold, sternly I told him in one ear, "I am only here to help you!"

Releasing my bear hug, I aggressively grabbed an arm and twisted it around his back toward his tangled messy curly blond hair. In a calmer voice I told him, "You are coming back with me!"

With the normal sound of the city reappearing in my awareness, I recall being surprised that McFly did not utter a word and went limp like a rag doll. All his flight energy was gone. Without a firm hold of his twisted arm, he would have crumpled to the ground.

Trying to make eye contact from behind him, I gazed upon a very weak, desperate, and lonely person. I told him, "Hey man, I do not want to see you go back to the Lane!"

While standing in the garden, I tried to assure him. "There is nowhere else to go."

With the chase over, I gently released my grasp. While shaking the flow of blood back into my arm, I trailed McFly as we retraced our path through the gardens. Once free, side by side, we meandered back to Region 5.

Again back through the security door, we sat quietly in the round room until his parole officer arrived. McFly did not utter a word.

The round room was used for reentry meetings after students were expelled or suspended. It was quiet and secluded from the classrooms down the hall.

With Robert Smalls' arrival, I could sense by his facial expression that he was amazed that we had taken the time to chase down McFly. With McFly indirectly listening, I explained, "We all like McFly, and we do not want to see him go back to Maple Lane."

The image of McFly needing cigarettes made me cringe.

Smalls knew McFly's history, and as we shook hands, his body language showed his appreciation.

Once McFly's group home supervisor arrived, I left the room.

Several minutes later, Roman entered the building huffing and puffing. Looking at him reminded me that I had totally forgotten about the other runner. I could tell by the look on Roman's face that he had gotten away. I asked, "Who was that guy?"

Roman simply said, "He is a new student, and I am not sure who he is."

Assuming that McFly's running partner was from the group home, I reentered the round room, "You have another runner on your hands."

The group home supervisor was surprised. After a quick phone call, they replied, "Everyone except McFly is accounted for at the group home."

Puzzled, I asked McFly, "Who was that guy that ran with you?"

McFly, with his head lowered, meekly shrugged. "I don't know."

It turned out that the second runner did not know McFly either. Apparently, he just ran for the fun of it. To this day, I do not remember who this guy was. It is quite possible that this runner never returned to Region 5. He was probably a new student, and he decided that it would be exciting to run from the building.

This incident reminds me that many of our students got caught up in criminal situations without realizing what they were doing or what the consequences would be. Whether a passenger in a drive-by shooting or unknowingly standing next to an acquaintance during a strong-armed robbery, some kids are just at the wrong place at the wrong time and make poor decisions.

For some reason, Region 5 was not the right fit for McFly's running partner. As a result, he took the excitement of the opportunity to run, not even knowing who McFly was.

McFly was not sent back to Maple Lane, and he continued to attend Region 5 and live at the group home.

29. Recognition

Ax Slayer Nominated for

BOYS CLUB HALL OF FAME

When we, the teachers at Region 5 Learning Center found out that our secretary had nominated Clark for this award, we were outraged at her callous stupidity.

Generally reeking of the previous night's alcohol and cigarettes, our secretary at the time had taken it upon herself to nominate Clark for the award. As a result, for weeks we had reporters and prank phone callers trying to get information about Clark.

Our current secretary, Alice, had absolutely no idea the pain and humiliation that she put Clark through. She did not even work with Clark. She had no clue regarding his progress other than he got straight-A grades. What a drunken fool she proved to be.

Expecting the potential for media madness, Roman and I got creative. We were not going to allow the media to get to Clark. For several weeks, after the hall of fame nomination fiasco, we would back the school van up to the back doors of the building and sneak Clark away.

One day I recall clearly. After returning from life sports, there was a news media van in our parking lot and a reporter hanging around on the sidewalk waiting for school to get out.

Before we arrived back from life sports, Roman unsuccessfully attempted to contact our principal Mack and Clark's father. Both were unavailable. Not having experience with the media, we were on our own.

After the Platoon and I exited the school van, body blocking the reporter's access to our students, I calmly informed him, "You are out of line for trying to interview our students."

Ignoring me, he continued attempts to interview students about Clark. Surprisingly, they had nothing to do with him.

Again requesting that the reporter leave, he boldly proclaimed, "The sidewalk is public property, and I will stay here as long as I want."

In a stare-down that no one won, I directed him, "You better move your media van out of our parking lot or I will call the police and have it towed!"

Stubbornly complying and not too happy, Mr. Media asked his driver to leave our parking lot, and strode right back to his sidewalk position.

Once the students were dismissed and were out of sight, reentering the building, sensing a conflict with Mr. Media, Roman suggested, "I will handle the reporter while you get Clark out the back door."

Roman was generally more rational about situations. I was usually the emotional one, he was more methodical.

Roman had graduated with a four-point GPA from the University of Washington in Seattle. He is a very intelligent man. I will always be impressed that he bypassed law school to be a teacher. He wanted to make a difference in his community as an educator, rather than as an attorney.

Splitting off, while Roman distracted Mr. Media on the sidewalk, I quickly slid out the rear lunchroom door. Not attracting attention, I backed the van up to the adjacent emergency exit. The exit doors were at the end of the U-shape that made up the structure of the Region 5 building.

Through the rear view mirror, I watched as Clark crawled over the back seat. He looked relaxed, but concerned. I calmly informed him, "Clark, your dad can't be reached. Don't worry, we got this handled."

As we pulled out of the parking lot, I could see that Roman, arms crossed, was diplomatically as always, having a discussion with Mr. Media. He had tactically positioned himself during the conversation so that Mr. Media's back was facing the van's exit.

Roman's strategy worked; with Clark hidden in the back seat, we slipped out of the parking lot unnoticed.

To relieve the stress, Clark and I went out for hot fudge sundaes. Hot fudge sundaes always seem to melt away tensions.

Once parked, we enjoyed our fudge sundaes in silence. Clark knew why the media was dogging him, no need to talk about it. Strange, the staff was more upset at our smoke-smelling, last-night's-alcohol-breath secretary than he was. It gave me an odd feeling to see that he was more relaxed than I was.

There were no cell phones back in the day, none that I could afford anyway, so I could not call Clark's father to tell him where we were. After we exited the Region 5 parking lot, Roman ditched Mr. Media and eventually was able to leave a message at Clark's father's place of employment.

As soon as Clark's father became aware that the media was at Region 5, he left work and got there as quickly as possible. By the time he arrived, Mr. Media was gone. Roman, as always, filled in the gaps and settled him down.

When we reached Clark's house, I was surprised at its location. Clark must have sensed my lack of reaction and meekly said, "My dad sold his house for my defense."

I though it interesting that Clark had not said, "He sold *our* house."

Pausing to put together the right words, looking at the house, he said, "We are renting."

As we sat quietly in front of his house, I was surprised that Clark did not eagerly exit the van. It was almost as if he wanted to explain something to me. We were in an average-income area of Tacoma, and he seemed apprehensive.

Scanning the neighborhood, I recall that Clark's house was the best maintained. The lawn was mowed, hedges trimmed, and the sidewalk was edged. It was small, but very tidy.

Not making eye contact, Clark meekly repeated, "My dad sold his house for my defense."

Once again, Clark had not said, "He sold *our* home." Did I hear in his voice remorse—or did I?

As Clark exited the van, for reasons I cannot explain, I opened my door and quietly followed.

"This is our home," Clark said without making eye contact as we meandered to the front door.

As we got closer, I noticed the paint was slightly peeling away from the window wrappings. The front door had a broken pane of glass that fragmented out from the corner like a spider's wed.

Clark barely knocked on the door before it ripped open.

I vividly recall the relieved expression on Clark's father's face. Ignoring me, he gave Clark a tightly wrapped fatherly hug.

As time slowed, I barely noticed Clark's father freeing one arm to shake my hand. Making eye contact, reaching for the out-stretched gesture, I was struck at the firm shake and the roughness of his hand. I thought to myself, "This is a hard-working man. He is a worker, not a desk jockey."

Not being invited in, I quietly backed off as they entered their home.

Once back in the school van, fastening my seat belt, I took a second long look at the well-kept house and yard. I kept hearing Clark's words: "This is our home."

Feeling guilty for spinning gravel as I slipped away, I caught myself wondering, "What happened to this guy?"

To most people, this and other situations might seem like the entire staff at Region 5 was suffering from the Stockholm Syndrome.

It is weird to try and put yourself in the shoes of a kid like Clark. I knew he would probably end up in prison. Saddened by that fact, I tried not to dwell on the statistics that showed that most of our students were either going to Pierce County Jail or prison.

Reflecting back, we wanted to build our students' academic levels and self-esteem and give them some positive memories to build a solid life.

Regardless of Clark's crime, while he was at Region 5, he was treated the same as everyone else.

We just tried to, do the best, with what we had.

In America, you get second chances in life.

30. 8×10

I did not follow Clark's second trial. Roman did, and he filled me in on the details whenever I asked. I am sure Roman could sense the pain that I felt for Clark and did not openly talk about it to me.

Clark was a great kid, almost too perfect. He was almost flawless. I always thought, and still do even to this day, "Someone ground him into perfection, whether he wanted it or not."

The day that Clark pled guilty, it was all over the news. Several days later after he was sentenced, our day-after drunk secretary Alice spread the rumor that Clark had copped a plea and had been given fifteen years in prison.

As Alice slithered in and told me from across the staff room, I could almost smell her stinky breath. We did not get along very well. She was a back-stabber who always snitched to Mack whenever I bent the rules.

On that day, Roman and I were hanging around after school in the staff lounge. Watching the street people hopelessly wonder by, we had a clear vantage point of the front door.

I do not remember the reason we were there, maybe it was Clark's trial or maybe it was us once again trying to figure out what made good kids turn evil.

Being deep in conversation, we were startled by the entry security buzzer at the front door. In unison we looked up to see Clark's father with an elderly lady. I immediately recognized her as Clark's grandmother.

Emanating a shadow of gloom, they entered Region 5 being drawn toward us.

Grandma had puffy eyes, and it was obvious that she had been crying for some time. Clark's father, who had lost a lot of weight and showed it, just gave each of us a firm handshake.

After some small talk, Grandma handed me an 8×10 photo in a gold frame.

Bringing the conversation to a conclusion, she went on to thank us for all that we had done for Clark.

When she spoke, her eyes never left mine. It was as if Grandma was looking straight into my soul. "This was Clark's favorite photo, and he wanted us to give it to you," she said.

Tearing up, she went on, "He has a lot of respect for you."

Feeling like crying, I had been wrongly taught at an early age that men do not cry and held it in. Being deeply touched by her words, I gave her a hug.

There was a thank you card along with the photo. I barely read it being hypnotized by the photograph.

Not keeping the card, I kept the photo and have it to this day. The gold-framed photo was posted with pride right behind my desk until a short-sighted assistant superintendent decided to relocate Region 5 Learning Center.

The photo was of Clark, Smiley, and me kneeling on the frozen water of Lake George.

Of all the photos taken of Clark snowshoeing, hiking, mountain biking, and other road trips, he chose this photo to frame and give to me.

I wonder why?

31. Sausage Gravy over Spuds

several "man time" years later, while my parents and I were having breakfast at the Ram Restaurant on 26th and North Pearl Street, I had an interesting experience.

After enjoying a large plate of specially requested sausage gravy over hash browns, the waitress was slower than usual in bringing us our bill. Loving an early morning breakfast and good conversation, I was not too concerned. After a longer than usual period, I motioned to the waitress.

Pausing, taking her time, the skinny little waitress tilted her head, glanced toward the bar and said, "He paid for your meal." Acting overly busy, almost grunting, she marched off.

Swinging my thoughts toward the bar, I recognized Clark's father. With a drink in one hand and a smoke in the other, with a half smile, he raised his glass and nodded.

After motioning to my parents, we walked over to him. "Thanks. That was not necessary."

With cigarette smoke escaping from his smile, Clark's father slowly responded, "When I am in the same restaurant as you, you will never pay for a meal."

Taking another drag, he appeared to have snuck down more than one early morning cocktail. "Clark will never forget you and neither will I," he said in a respectful manner.

"You gave him a fair shake, and that's all we could ask."

Pausing, lost for words, to get my brain back to work, I finally introduced my parents.

After pleasantries, Clark's father explained, "Clark had some great adventures at Region 5, and it helped him through some tough times."

As Clark's father was expressing his appreciation, it gave me a warm feeling for my parents to be there.

Reflecting back to our chance encounter, it was ironic for our fathers to be face to face. If not for my father, who'd exposed me to the outdoors, I would not have exposed Clark to challenging outdoor adventures.

Unconsciously, I passed on to the Region 5 students, what I learned from my parents. Sports, hiking, snowshoeing, mountain-biking, and other outdoor activities. These activities helped me to be a healthier person and enjoy life.

Subconsciously, I guess, I just wanted to pass on it on to those less fortunate.

I also tried to apply what Margaret once told me: "Darrell, do whatever you can, nothing else has worked with these kids."

In the long-term scheme of personal growth, it is the exposure to healthy activities and a change of thought patterns that modifies behaviors. As humans, we can change our bad habits, by consciously changing our thoughts.

Clark's father finished his conversation with a handshake that needed no further words of thanks.

I did not ask about Clark. I knew he was in prison, but that was it. I figured that if his father wanted to talk about it, he would have brought it up. I could see in his eyes that he was hurting; who wouldn't be in a situation like his.

We left the restaurant with a comforting feeling.

Sad for Clark and his father, I felt that we had done our job.

Our job was not to judge, but to provide an educational setting for all to grow academically and personally.

32. D.O.C.

I am not sure how many years passed after running into Clark's father when it happened, but Clark gave me a call.

Upon reflection, I almost did not answer the phone. The caller ID read Department of Correction, D.O.C. I never take calls from prison or jail, and I tell my students that I live in Gig Harbor not Tacoma.

Receiving the call from Clark, I was in the process of refinishing the attic in our house. As I recall, I was right in the middle of building a knee-wall out of 2×6 wood studs and felt disturbed by the interruption.

As my cell phone buzzed over and over like a dog yapping for a treat, for some reason I followed my instincts.

Hesitantly, I pushed the talk button not knowing who it could be. The unidentified person on the other end started talking to me as if we were old friends. I could tell by the way he communicated with ease that he knew me and was comfortable in conversation.

At first I played it off as if I knew whom I was talking to. Stalling and trying my hardest to place the voice to a face on the other end, I was at a loss.

"You don't know who this is, do you?" the unknown voice asked after a pause.

Sheepishly I responded, "No, I'm sorry. I don't know who this is."

In a man's voice, he echoed, "It is Clark."

After a long silence, lost for words, I asked, "Where are you? You don't sound the same."

With a dead flat tone Clark replied, "Prison will do that to you."

As we were talking, a weird thought crept into my mind. What if he asks about Smiley?

In the end, I was glad that he didn't. I hated withholding the truth, but I would have with that horrible story, for his sanity and mine.

I remember feeling no fear regarding Clark calling me. I was glad to hear that he was at the halfway house next to Remann Hall. I commented in a questioning tone, "I am surprised that I haven't seen you, I walk the students from the Day Reporting School to the bus stop every day."

After a pause, Clark changed the subject, dodging my question. I did not pursue a response. He must have been avoiding the subject for a reason.

Clark and I exchanged more small talk and reminisced about our adventures at Region 5. I said, even though I was unsure if it would happen, "We should get together, maybe for breakfast?"

Exchanging contact information, I sensed that we both knew that a reunion was not forth coming.

Happy that he was alive, I could tell that prison life had taken all the youth out of him. Clark sounded hollow and that worried me.

Being in the unfinished attic when he called, I remember writing his number on the only thing available at the time, a 2×6 wood stud. Weird, once I thought about looking for his number, I remembered vividly the eight-foot stud that I'd written it on. The problem was, I could not remember where I'd used it as part of the knee- wall framing to our attic.

Odd, the only connection to Clark that I had, his phone number, is part of the wood structure of our family attic.

Tucked safely behind the primed and painted sheetrock was Clark's name and phone number.

In retrospect, maybe I was afraid to see what prison life had done to him. Working with court-connected students for as long as I have, I made it a practice not to pursue relationships after they left. Sadly, hard for me to face, some of our students ended up in Pierce County Jail or hooked into the revolving adult prison system.

I could have found Clark if I'd wanted to.

Not pursuing a reunion, I wanted to remember him as he once was.

33. Follower

Several years before Clark's unexpected call, we had just moved into the house that we are currently living in when I was caught off guard one evening by something I saw on the television.

Relaxing with my son Drake on my lap, barely watching the five-o-clock evening news, I saw it out of the corner of my eye. It was like driving down a mountain highway and observing a deer out of your peripheral vision hidden in the trees. Anticipating it leaping into your vehicle, your heart rate automatically increases.

For only a moment, I thought that I recognized a behavioral gesture by the masked robbery suspect on the television screen. Concentrating more on the many projects that the house needed done, I was watching, but barely listening to the details of the crime.

Hearing bits and pieces about an armed robbery in the city of Lakewood, Washington, slow creeping goose bumps overtook possession of my skin.

Watching, almost missing it, a lengthy shadowy blur of video surveillance from the robbery momentarily popped on the screen again. Sitting back, as I absent-mindedly hugged Drake, a weird feeling came over me.

Unable to get the visual out of my mind, switching to several other news channels trying to catch another glimpse of the robbery suspect, I was deprived.

Haunted, I patiently stayed awake to watch the eleven-o-clock presentation of the same newscast. While waiting, there was something in the suspected armed robber's quirky movements that kept emerging from my subconscious.

Watching the news again, with the only light in the room emanating from the television, I was at full attention. Analyzing the perpetrator's every body movement, I was convinced.

Stunned, sitting alone, pointing to the image, I blurted out to no one but myself, "I know you!"

Fiercely trying to remember, leaning forward on the couch, I recognized the weird mannerisms of the robbery suspect. He had a jerky weird sort of movement. When he moved, his shoulders seemed to rotate up and down in an awkward motion. The tilt of his head and his awkward walk were hauntingly familiar.

Breaking away from the television, creeping silently into bed, wrestling to capture sleep, I could not place the weird body movements to a face, but I was convinced that I knew him.

Several days after I had stashed the visual image of the surveillance video away in the back of my mind, Robert Smalls popped into Region 5 Learning Center unexpectedly.

While sitting in the staff lounge, positioned to watch anyone coming or going from the building, I noticed that Smalls was not wearing his usual gleaming smile. Once buzzed in through the security door, ignoring everyone else, Smalls marched directly toward me.

Standing at attention, making eye contact, he asked, "Did you see him on TV?"

Without another word, it hit me like an impending car wreck. Bringing everything to a slowing reality, speechless, I did not quickly respond.

As visual snap-shots quickly emerged from the depths of my memories, I visualized Smalls warming the robbery suspect's sockless frozen feet in his armpits.

His crooked stroke-victim smile emerged in my thoughts like the face of a long lost friend.

Dumbstruck, after time resumed its normal momentum, without making eye contact, shaking my head, I finally responded, "I knew, watching those weird body movements that I knew who it was."

"He will go to the big house for this one" was Small's solemn response.

Feeling Smalls' eyes burning into my soul, turning to face my friend, I shared what we both knew. "He will not do well there."

Several days later, sitting in the Region 5 staff lounge, Roman quietly handed me the front page article regarding McFly's capture and attempted murder charges.

Side-stepping the article, I was mesmerized by McFly's tilted head and crooked smile captured by his mug shot photo. For days I refused to look at the many photo poster boards of McFly's adventures as a platoon member. I could not come to grips with his smiling image and the gloomy prospect of life as a prisoner.

When McFly left Region 5, not keeping in contact with him, we were told, turning eighteen and not eligible for state services, he lived on the streets. Region 5 was a transition program; we did not graduate students. He was one of many students whom we tried to put back on the right track.

Of the thousands of students that I have worked with, for some reason, McFly has always stood out.

Once at home that afternoon, I sat quietly in my car pondering McFly's manipulated decisions. After several minutes, feeling depressed, I slowly emerged and paused. Leaning on the front hood for support, glanced up at our new home, I thought, "What a wreck!"

My inner voice echoed, "What a waste of time to spend thirteen months fighting against twenty-seven lien-holders to get this beat up old house!"

At the time, the lawn and fruit trees surrounding the house were wildly overgrown with curling nasty sticker bushes. The windows above the sagging balcony were peeling paint and droopy. The rotted balcony was crooked and warped on one end like a mocking smile with broken teeth. The interior was even worse—nothing was consistent. There was missing wood trim and the wood floors were marred almost beyond repair.

Everything about the house seemed abused and used up.

Almost in conversation with the house, I said aloud, "In 1898, when you were constructed, you must have been the beauty of the neighborhood."

Gazing at the abused house, popping off to no one but myself, I said aloud, "After years of neglect and abuse, you're in horrible condition."

Pondering the "what-ifs", I felt sympathy for the old tattered house.

Submissively, similar to subliminal pop and candy messages mixed into the old real to real movies frames, McFly immerged in my private thoughts.

The tattered old faded yellow house was similar to that of McFly's journey through life.

"What-if................."

34. Disconnection

I have to wonder, what could have been done to save McFly? While he was at Region 5 Learning Center he was at his best. Similar to McFly, most of our court-connected students were fourteen or fifteen—ninth graders when they became involved in drugs, gangs and crime. The pre-1980s junior high school system provided more avenues to better prepare students for the stresses of the high school system.

In my opinion, the majority of ninth-grade students today are too young and unprepared for high school.

I can reflect back to when McFly showed great determination while hiking along the snow cover trail to frozen Lake George. His toes could have had frostbite and he would not have given up. How could we as a society have corralled that determination into a positive force?

McFly had a lot to deal with at an early age and couldn't seem to shake his past. Yes, I place most of the blame on his low-life scumbag parents. If they had been decent, his life would have been different.

With the lack of parenting in mind, we must ask ourselves, if parents are not doing their job, do we as a society have the obligation to care for their children? Is it our responsibility to take the parent role?

I believe to save kids, we must accept that responsibility. The school system is the perfect venue to teach discipline, morality, honor, and life skills.

We all know that most troubled students have a horrible home life.

Let us stop using that as an excuse. Based upon what I have experienced, across the nation, in urban school districts, we need to return to the junior high school system and create avenues for students to connect and be successful. Ninth graders are too young and unprepared for high school.

The structure of the group home, guidance from Robert Smalls, and people caring kept McFly out of trouble, keeping evil at bay. That structure could have been provided before McFly ended up being manipulated into committing armed robbery and attempted murder.

McFly is just a number now, a non-entity. Could his house, his core, have been rebuilt?

It is obvious that McFly was not the mastermind of the robbery. He was too simple a thinker for that. He was susceptible to suggestions and manipulation.

Having no idea if McFly is still in prison or where he is, I would like to find out.

Being very disappointed in McFly's decisions, I had hoped that we made a difference with him, but apparently we were too late.

35. Green Eyes

Eight years after McFly's conviction, Region 5 Learning Center occurrences continue to resurface.

Several weeks ago, I was moving several boxes of books from my bedroom closet to the basement. While taking a break from walking up and down two flights of stairs, I was drawn to a dusty old book that had fallen out of one of the boxes. Out of place, it was lying alone on the bare wood floor.

Reaching, I awkwardly grabbed the book by the cover only. As the pages fanned out, like a pressed flower placed between the pages, a finely flattened news article eased out from hiding.

Glancing at the neatly folded article on the floor; unlike a colorfully pressed spring flower, death seemed to emanate from its torn edges.

Hesitating, I sensed the evil information begging to be released.

Squatting on one knee and leaning over, I pinched the article's edges with my thumb and index finger to separate it from the floor. Gently picking it up, I unfolded the faded yellowing news clip. The article described the murder of two former Region 5 students, Crispus Hamton and Anthony Gray.

It was a common story, two more Original Gangsters (OG's) dead.

Given the experiences that I have had with troubled youth, I believe that Crispus could have been saved if the junior high system had not been replaced by the middle school system in the early 1980s.

The Crip and Blood gangs' steamrolled into Tacoma at the same time the transition to the middle school system and the elimination of afterschool extracurricular activities occurred.

If sports had been available rather than gangs, Crispus might have gotten into sports or other extracurricular activities. Unfortunately for nice impressionable guys like Crispus, they had nothing to do after school and rambled around looking for something to belong to. Gangs filled that need.

Reading the article, I thought about Crispus' sparkling green eyes. While at Region 5, he was a happy carefree individual. At age fourteen or fifteen, he was not your typical wanna-be gang member. He may have claimed to be a banger, but at school he never harassed rival gang members and was eager to learn new things. His smile was an open invitation to a joke or good conversation.

After pondering the waste of his murder again, I continue to wonder, could the Tacoma Schools have saved Crispus?

The even larger question is, what could our community have done to prevent Crispus from connecting to a life of crime at an early age and eventually being murdered?

Crime Stoppers Tacoma/Pierce County

UNSOLVED HOMICIDES- 2001

Victims Crispus Hamton and Anthony Gray

Pierce County Sheriff's detectives need your help to identify the suspect responsible for the murder of Crispus Hamton and Anthony Gray.

At 10:20p.m. on May 24th, 2001, victims Crispus Hamton and Anthony Gray were shot to death by an unidentified suspect as the victims were inside of a truck parked in the 18500 block of 14th Ave. E in Spanaway. At the time of the homicide, the victim's maroon and gray 1980 Ford Ranger had the engine running and the headlights were turned on.

Detectives believe the unidentified suspect was seated in the back seat of the truck, and shot both victims from behind. The suspect then fled the vehicle and was heard running through the bushes. It is also believed that the victims may have been attempting to illegally purchase firearms from the suspect at the time.

Many school districts across the nation changed to middle schools in the early 1980s. I believe that this transition is partly responsible for the gang activities and high dropout rate in our country.

In addition, to save money, school districts cut extracurricular programs. This short-sighted decision left kids, like Crispus, with nothing to do after school.

Not having after school activities left many vulnerable students disconnected and susceptible to drugs, gangs and crime.

36. Blue and Red

After stumbling across Crispus' article, I had another weird incident occur. Not really sure how we got going on the topic, I usually never talk about former Region 5 Learning Center students with the current students at the Remann Hall Day Reporting School. I have no idea whose parent or relative I may have known who is now dead or in prison.

I have been working with kids on parole or probation for twenty-three years. Interesting, my journey back to Region 5 involves many incidents with gang students of the 23rd Street Hilltop Crips, coincidence?

The gang-connected students whom I worked with at Region 5 are now in their thirties or forties, if alive.

In class that particular day, I had four Hilltop Crips or descendents of Hilltop Crips. Their names were Crispus, Deonte, Chaser, and Jaylee. I found it an odd coincidence that one of them was named Crispus and pursued my curiosity.

The conversation went something like this:

Mr. Hamlin: Crispus, who were you named after?

Crispus: Why?

Mr. Hamlin: In the twenty-three years that I have taught, I have only known two guys named Crispus.

Deonte (a new student): You have done this for twenty-three years!

Chaser: Twenty-third—I love that number.

Mr. Hamlin: Chaser, save it! No, I taught for fifteen years on the Hill at a school called Region 5 Learning Center. For the last eight years, I have taught here at the Day Reporting School.

Chaser: Mr. Hamlin knows my whole family.

Mr. Hamlin: Crispus, were you named after someone else?

Crispus: I got it from my uncle.

Mr. Hamlin: Your mother had a brother? Was he your mom's blood brother?

Crispus: No, I think he was my father's brother.

Chaser: I'm related to Crispus. He's my uncle.

Crispus: Mr. Hamlin had my mom as a student.

Chaser: Zantha was a student of yours?

Mr. Hamlin: Yes. She was smart like Crispus.

Crispus: I was named after my uncle that was killed.

Mr. Hamlin: Was his last name Hamton?

Crispus: I think so…yeah, that was it.

Mr. Hamlin: Do you know how he was killed?

Crispus: Someone killed him. I was real small so I don't remember.

Mr. Hamlin: Do you want to know?

Crispus: I went to his funeral, but I was too small to remember.

Mr. Hamlin: I knew your uncle well. I can still see his light green eyes in my memory.

Chaser: Did you know my dad?

Mr. Hamlin: It seems like I know the entire Washington family. Crispus! Please stop drumming. I can't hear Chaser over it.

Crispus: My bad.

Jaylee: Do you know my uncle Capone?

Mr. Hamlin: What is his birth name?

Jaylee: I don't know. I only know him by Capone.

Crispus: What do you know about my uncle?

Mr. Hamlin: Years after he left Region 5 he was assassinated with a friend of his, I knew both of them.

Crispus: What do you mean?

Mr. Hamlin: Your uncle Crispus was in Lakewood near the Army base trying to buy automatic weapons. He was shot in the back of the head.

Crispus: That must have been why there was a lump on the front of his head at the funeral. I was only three or four, but I remember that.

Chaser: The bullet must have gone right through the back of his head and out the front.

Mr. Hamlin: I don't know anything about that.

Crispus: I remember now, my mom said he was shot in the head.

Jaylee: No wonder he was killed, buying that.

Mr. Hamlin: Crispus, all that I can tell you is, your uncle was a good man and I was very sad when he was murdered.

Chaser: Did you go to the funeral?

Mr. Hamlin: I've had so many students killed, that it is too sad for me to go to their funerals.

Chaser: Did you know my dad Chaser Washington?

Mr. Hamlin: I am not sure. I knew your uncle and aunt. Remember, I showed you the inner-tubing photo of when I took them to Mount Rainier National Park. Your uncle snuck in the HTC sign in our group photo. He was lucky that I didn't see it at the time.

Chaser: My dad said I am twice as bad as him.

Mr. Hamlin: I don't know how you are on the outs, but in here, you're a smart hard-working student. You're lucky that you can read so well.

Chaser: My dad said he was in a lot of fights at Jason Lee.

Mr. Hamlin: I do not know about that. I just do not remember him being at Region 5. I do remember Big Granny. If I remember correctly, she was the oldest of the Washington kids. She loved to be in the mountains. Your uncle Nathan was quiet, rarely ever talked. He was the youngest I believe.

Chaser: He's doing thirty years because of some snitches.

Mr. Hamlin: I was sad to see his photo in the paper. The Feds got a lot of my old students.

Chaser: The Feds were everywhere. They tried to get Big Granny.

Mr. Hamlin: I knew a lot of those original gangsters, the O.G.s.

Jaylee: Who else do you know?

Mr. Hamlin: Do you know Jammer?

Jaylee: He is my uncle.

Mr. Hamlin: Is he related to the Daltons?

Chaser: The Daltons are related to the McCoys. My aunt married a Dalton.

Mr. Hamlin: Whatever happened to Jammer?

Jaylee: He's in prison somewhere.

Mr. Hamlin: He was one of the most talented basketball players I ever saw.

Chaser: Not in prison he ain't.

Mr. Hamlin: What about the Jeffersons, do you know them?

Chaser: The McCoys, Daltons, and Jeffersons are all related.

Mr. Hamlin: Where are they now?

Chaser: Dead or in prison.

Mr. Hamlin: I knew a lot of the red and blue guys from the eighties and nineties.

Crispus: My mom was a Crip. She ran the Puyallup Fair.

Mr. Hamlin: Ask your mom about the thick black Puyallup Fair markers.

Crispus: You know I don't see my mom!

Mr. Hamlin: Crispus, I'm sorry. I didn't remember that.

Crispus: If you want to see my mom, go to her church on the Hill.

Chaser: Do you go to church?

Mr. Hamlin: I should go to church after working with court connected kids for twenty-three years.

Deonte: You worked here for twenty-three years?

Chaser: Notice, twenty-third!

Mr. Hamlin: Chaser let it go.

Chaser: My bad.

Crispus: What about the markers?

Mr. Hamlin: Well, back in the day, the blue guys would park in the blue parking lot and the red guys would park in the red parking lot. Once they entered the red or blue entrance gate, they would meet inside of the Puyallup Fairgrounds and fight.

Jaylee: Now I know what you mean by the blue guys.

Chaser: The Crips are blue, the Bloods are red.

Mr. Hamlin: Anyway, the red and blue guys would go inside the fair and start brawling with each other.

Crispus: I heard about that. There were snipers on the rooftops ready to kill gangsters.

Mr. Hamlin: No, those guys were the spotters. When the gangsters started fighting, the police spotters would notify other officers and they would swoop in deep and get them out of the fair.

Chaser: Yeah, but they could just get back in.

Mr. Hamlin: Crispus, ask your mom about it.

Crispus: What are you saying?

Mr. Hamlin: Sorry, calm down. I worked security at the time and I saw your mom's photograph with a huge black X on her hand.

Crispus: I told you she was a Crip.

Chaser: What?

Mr. Hamlin: If the bangers, red or blue, were kicked out of the fair, the police marked a huge thick X on their hand.

Chaser: So they couldn't get back in?

Mr. Hamlin: Crispus, I can't hear Chaser if you're drumming and singing.

Crispus: My bad.

Deonte: You have done this for twenty-five years?

Chaser: He said twenty-three for Twenty-Third Street Hilltop Crips.

Mr. Hamlin: Okay Chaser, thanks to you, we are done talking about this. Enough of this talk. Let's get back to your lesson.

Chaser: Who else do you know?

Mr. Hamlin: Chaser, another day, let it go, ok?

I tried to remember the conversation as best as I could. The conversation would not have happened if there were descendants of red guys in the classroom. It is quite possible that their relatives may have been involved in shootings, beatings, or stabbings with each other.

This was a rare opportunity, and when we started talking, I had no idea where the conversation was going.

37 A Shadow

T hat same day, as I walked the Day Reporting School students to the bus stop to make sure that they did not fight or smoke weed, the fresh air did not diminish my growing mood of despair. Bits and pieces of our conversation in the classroom were reemerging over and over again like a broken record.

After watching the students safely get on the Pierce Transit bus, I found a quiet secluded spot to sit and think. Watching traffic go by while sitting on the gray retaining wall next to the 6th Avenue entrance to Remann Hall, I was contemplating my conversation with the second generation of Hilltop Crips.

Questioning myself, I asked, "Did anything that we did at Region 5 make a bit of difference?"

While sitting on the retaining wall feeling sorry for myself, I did not notice a tall man approach until his shadow blocked my warmth from the afternoon sun. Staring off in the direction of the long-vanished Pierce Transit bus, I was lost in my thoughts until he was standing right over me.

"You don't remember me, do you?" a quiet voice said from above.

Looking up, using my hand to block the sun, it was his smile that I noticed first.

Startled and trying not to show it, I quickly stood up to face him on even ground. The way the day was going, I had a passing thought: "I hope this guy isn't pissed off at me for something from the past."

Without introductions, in an awkward motion he held out his hand. Surprised, I instinctively reached out and shook his extended gesture.

As casual as if we talked daily, he said, "I have passed here several times on the bus and wanted to stop and talk to you. I live with my aunt just down the street."

He turned and pointed west in the direction of the Tacoma Narrows Bridge.

"Coming out of Maple Lane, I did not know what to expect. You guys really helped me out."

As he expressed himself, the gleaming smile never left his face.

Continuing to share his thoughts, it was like watching a smiling car salesman on TV. I have always been amazed that sales people can carry on an entire conversation with a smile; he was doing it while asking for nothing in return.

His smile was infectious; before I knew it, I was smiling too. His smile was a gift, a glow of inspiration that overshadowed a depressing afternoon.

"Well, I better get going," he said, again holding out his hand like a man.

"It's been real nice seeing you."

Watching him turn and proudly walk away, I barely said a word during the conversation.

As he strode off in the direction of his aunt's house, I thought, "Weird, another Region 5 student has emerged."

I caught myself wondering in disappointment, "What was his name?"

Sitting back down on the cement retaining wall, smiling, while watching his silhouette diminish in size, a thought passed before me; "Why didn't I ask for his name and number?"

38. Mount Si

U nexpectedly, my journey back in time to Region 5 Learning Center continued to evolve. One Saturday afternoon while cleaning out a cubby hole in my basement, an odd-shaped cardboard box attracted my attention.

Almost ready to toss it into a large black industrial garbage bag, I noticed a disheveled curling stack of old photos. Looking in, at the top of the stack, popping out and hoping to be seen, members of the North Star Platoon were proudly standing at the top Mount Si.

"Here we go again," I thought.

The Mount Si trailhead is located about forty minutes from Tacoma, just off Interstate 90 toward Snoqualmie Pass. I do not remember the year, but Mount Si was another challenging trek that I liked to take with the North Star Platoon.

We began our hike just outside the town of North Bend. Mount Si is an excellent challenge for hikers to achieve a priceless view of Seattle and the Seattle Space Needle. The round-trip hike is about ten miles and tough. This is not a beginner's hike.

On this particular day, I had more than a dozen platoon members.

One of the students on the trip was named Earl. He was a quiet tough guy. His real name was Earl G. Turner. During his enrollment, he did not say a single word about our strict dress code or behavior contract. The quiet students, like Earl, who attended Region 5 Learning Center were the ones that I worried about the most.

In the beginning, I did not trust Earl. He seemed institutionalized, which meant that he felt more comfortable being locked up than free. Often times juveniles will set themselves up to be arrested and locked back up. Sadly, the confines of a cell and the structure of a prison setting are safer to them, than the streets.

Earl had those sneaky eyes that were always looking around to see if anyone was watching him. He was living at a group home which led me to believe that his home life was unstable.

Admittedly during Earl's enrollment, I was concerned for the safety of myself and others. He looked cold and shifty. It was almost a week before he smiled or showed any emotion. I thought that he was a psychopath with no feeling at all.

Earl also did not like to be touched. Once, noticing him struggling with the educational software Word Grubber, I gently placed my hand on his shoulder to recognize his efforts. He reacted as if he had been assaulted, jumping out of his seat and in attacked mode.

Earl taught me a valuable lesson; do not touch wounded students, ever.

Another hiker that day was Josie. He had sad eyes and appeared to have had a rough life. Not remembering why he was attending Region 5, I do recall that he was tall, lean, and reminded me of a distance runner. Not wanting to be involved in the life sports program, he asked if he could go on the Mount Si hike anyway.

Josie explained, "I don't like hiking, but I really just want to get out of town."

I appreciated his honesty.

Looking at Josie, I explained, "I don't know you very well." Gazing into his sad eyes, I asked, "Can I trust you?"

Making eye contact, Josie responded, "Yes."

Pausing and trying to detect the honesty that he was conveying, I just said, "You're in." He appeared to have the makeup of a good athlete and could physically handle the hike. When I asked him about it, he calmly shared, "I never played sports."

One of the other Learning Center platoon members was Juan; he was a tough guy. He was another one of the quiet students that you could tell by looking into his eyes that he was a scrapper.

Usually quiet, when we were studying the Aztecs, Juan proclaimed, "I am a descendent of the Aztecs." No one even looked at him when he said it.

Caught by surprise, I explained to the students, "If Cortez had landed in Tabasco, Mexico, the year before or the year after 1519, he would have been smoked at the beach."

Interrupting, Juan blurted out, "I am happy that Hernando Cortez conquered the Aztecs." Juan's opinion caught me off guard and was contrary to what I had been taught.

Pausing again, taking this as a learning opportunity, I explained to the group, "European diseases actually killed most of the Aztecs, not the Spanish sword." I further stated, "Cortez was mistaken for the Aztec god Quatzicotle who was supposed to arrive in the year 1519."

Without raising his hand, Juan added, "The God was half man, half beast."

Being very impressed, I did not discourage Juan's interruptions.

"Cortez and the Spanish brought the first horses to America," proclaimed Juan with more students paying attention. He went on to explain, "When Cortez and his two hundred men rode their horses they looked like huge scary beasts."

Silently, maybe in fear, everyone appeared to be impressed with what Juan had to say and so was I.

Later that day, eating lunch with the students as usual, I asked Juan, "Why are you happy that Cortez defeated the Aztecs?"

Surprised, as if it were a simple concept, Juan explained, "The Aztecs were evil bloodthirsty beasts, and Cortez freed us."

"I'd never looked at the situation from that perspective. I appreciate you teaching me that."

Juan paused, looked at me as if I were simple in the head, and without saying a word nodded and went back to eating his school-district-prepared sack lunch.

Reflecting back on Juan, he was shorter than most of the other students, but made up for his height with Aztec courage. When he played basketball, volleyball, or pickle ball, unskilled as he was, he played to the maximum. Asking him about sports he said, "I love soccer, and played on a team before hitting the weed."

Feeling sorry for him, I did not doubt his story. Most likely, Juan had started smoking weed with the neighborhood gangbangers when he was twelve or thirteen. As a result, he had given up sports. It was the same story, different kid.

Also on the hike was Brant. He was one of those students that I could not figure out why he was at Region 5. Unless a student gave me trouble, I never read their file. Most students' pasts were a mystery to me.

Brant was a nice young man and did not give anyone grief. Doing his daily assignments, he was extremely cooperative. It was odd though—everyone seemed to be Brant's friend. He loved sports and quickly earned his way into the life sports program. Mount Si was Brant's first hike, and he was excited.

As usual, before we left Region 5, as students entered the school van, I searched pockets and patted the students down. I also looked through their backpacks to make sure there was nothing stashed inside. The Tacoma School District provided sack lunches for the field trip, so they did not have to worry about food. I did suggest that platoon members bring extra drinks for the hike.

Once at the Mount Si trailhead, I gave specific instructions to stay on the trail. I also told them to never drink water from streams. Explaining to the group, "Beaver fever would mean that you will spend the rest of your evening on the toilet with diarrhea."

Looking into their eyes, I could only assume that they knew that I was serious. In addition, I added, "Do not cut the switchbacks!" I was adamant and stressed to stay on the trail to protect the plants.

About a mile, maybe two miles into the hike I began to smell some remnants of marijuana. Coming upon the first group, I noticed that Earl was bent over looking at something.

"Is he stoned?" was my initial impression.

Surprising, Earl was smiling and seemed like a different person. "He must be stoned?" I thought without accusing. As he was bent over analyzing some ferns, this was the first time that I had seen Earl's huge beautiful smile.

Still not fully trusting Earl, as I got closer to him, pretending to trip, I leaned into him to get a good whiff. Nothing, Earl was clean, and I felt some pride knowing that he was trustworthy.

"Earl," I said, getting his attention after regaining my balance, "Do you know what that fern plant is used for?"

Earl just looked at me and didn't say a word. "If you happen to walk through poison ivy or have a rash, the back side of this plant will relieve the itching."

I pointed to the back of the fern. "All you have to do is rub the brown dots on the back side of this plant onto the rash."

Without a word, Earl ripped the fern leaf from the plant examining it.

"Earl, I know this is your first hike, but we do not rip out plants unless we need them." Without saying a word Earl got the message.

Surprising me, never having been hiking before, Earl had taken the leadership role of the group.

As usual with a large group, students were spread out along the five-mile trail to the summit hiking at different paces. I knew the students were safe—there was only one path that led to the top of Mount Si and they were on it.

Approaching the second group, again I leaned in pretending that I had lost my footing. I tried to catch a whiff of as many students as possible as I stumbled.

Yes, they were stoned.

As Juan was the leader of this group, looking at him square in the eyes I asked, "Is everything okay?"

Juan, not replying, just looked at me with expressionless glassed-over eyes. I gave him a look that said, "I know exactly what you have been doing."

Maintaining eye contact, I asked the small group, "What is that weird smell?" Without accusing anyone of anything and looking each platoon member in the eyes, I let them know that I knew exactly what they had done.

Picking up my pace, about four miles into the hike, I ran across Josie. He was hiking by himself, and I thought, "Why is this guy alone?" Then I remembered that before the hike, I hadn't told the platoon about the buddy system. I usually explained the Boy Scout law that says you must always have a hiking buddy.

Once upon Josie, I faked a stumble and leaned in for a whiff. Josie reached out and grabbed me, expecting me to fall.

Surprised, I looked at Josie's clear eyes and said, "Did you smell anything weird on the trail?"

Josie just looked at me, and I could tell in his eyes that he wanted to tell me, but could not.

I let it go, not wanting to put him in a compromising position. Happy that Josie was straight and had stayed true to his honor, patting him on the shoulder, I said, "Let's finish this together."

Once we got to the top of Mount Si, we looked around to find that no other platoon members were there. My first thoughts were, "These guys were so stoned that they fell off the mountain. I'm dead meat."

Glancing around, we were startled when several students popped out from behind huge boulders trying to scare us. Looking into their eyes, I could not tell if they were stoned or not. Without saying a word about being stoned I asked, "Where is everyone else?"

Looked up, speechless, they pointed to the top of the Mount Si stack.

Stunned, looking up at the steep cylindrical stack, I said out loud, "Oh my God, they did not go up there did they?"

Trying to gather my thoughts, giving Josie a trusting look, I said, "We better get up there and see what's going on."

Before Josie and I left to climb the backside of the Mt Si stack, I commanded the remaining group, "Make sure that no one else goes past this point!" To impress upon them the seriousness of the situation I sternly warned, "If anyone follows us up the stack, they will be emergency expelled!"

Adding, "I will personally call their probation officer too!" They got the point.

As Josie and I we climbing the backside of the Mount Si stack, I was very impressed at Josie's climbing abilities. Strangely, I had not thought twice about asking him to come along. As instructed, Josie followed my every hand and foot hold until we got to the top of the stack.

Once on top, I was amazed at how clear the view was of Seattle and the Space Needle. Being forty-five miles off in the distance, it was weird to be able to see them from the Stack. Mesmerized, most of my anger dissipated.

Scanning the top of the stack, I noticed that Brant and several other students were safe—what a relief.

So excited about the view, I could not bring myself to confront them about being stoned. To be honest, besides being stoned, I could not remember if I'd told them not to climb the stack. The hike and view of Seattle may well have been the highlight of their life.

Looking at them disappointedly, the excitement in their eyes exceeded my need for punishment.

Enjoying the view, we did not immediately descend from the Stack. It had been years since I'd been on top, and I was enjoying the view as much as they were. Emphasizing to the group that the view of Seattle was generally obscured by clouds, I added, "Being stoned does not increase the perception of the view."

With the exchange of eye contact, the group knew exactly what I was talking about. After sharing several minutes of the spectacular view and the accomplishment of climbing Mt. Si, we climbed down to the hook-up with the rest of the group.

While we were eating lunch, several of the students tried to engage me in conversation. Disappointed in the stoned students, I could barely think of anything else. I almost shouted, "How could you let me down like this? I am the only guy in the building that is willing to take the risk and expose you to new things!"

I felt trashed.

As always, the trip down was a lot easier than the trip up. Again, I emphasized, "There is to be no cutting the switchbacks. You all need to stay on the trail for safety." I had the feeling that after the weed-smoking incident, everyone would be compliant.

Once on the road, in the van with a captive audience, I tore into the group. I explained, "Your behaviors today are the reason why nobody wants to do anything for you!"

Stern, but not angry, I went on, "This is why people have given up on you!"

Driving at sixty-five miles an hour down Interstate 90, I wasn't looking at them as someone tried to interrupt me. Raising my voice to yell mode, I quickly told them, "Close your mouth and just listen!"

Angered now, I told the group, "We might as well call Region 5 the Last Chance Ranch!"

Looking in the mirror, I tried to make eye contact with as many of the platoon members as I could. "For some of you, this is your last chance!"

Letting the moment sink in, I followed up with, "How do you expect me to trust you, any of you, if you do me dirty like this!"

Not a word was spoken and no one asked to stop for hot fudge sundaes.

Eventually most of the platoon fell asleep giving me some quiet time to contemplate my next move.

I made no threats of calling probation officers or expulsions.

39. Honor

The next day after a sleepless night, before class started, several students approached me in private and told me who had provided the marijuana for the road trip to Mount Si. I was proud that students were stepping forward and showing some loyalty to the program.

Before lunch, looking around to make sure that no one was watching, Juan came up and said, "My bad for yesterday." He did not shake my hand and barely made eye contact before he turned and walked away.

"That is good enough for me," I thought without responding. I did not ask Juan who provided the weed. No need to test his loyalty to that degree.

Earl did not say a word about the incident and would barely make eye contact with me. I suspected that he was anticipating a suspension for being guilty by association. On the trail, I'd gotten a good whiff of Earl and knew that he was not involved. He would not give up the name either, so why ask.

Not blaming either of them for keeping quiet, there was no honor lost. They were products of the system. They lived by street law and street law usually prevailed. Earl dodged the temptation of smoking weed in favor of honor and that impressed me the most.

During life sports that day, I did not say a word about Mount Si. To be honest, I did not really know what to do. I did not want to suspend or expel the students for something they probably did with their parents. Many students through the years have shared with me that they began smoking weed with their parents or a relative.

Who am I to be the judge?

I just wanted their respect and honor when they were with me. They knew the rules. The honor system and the camaraderie that we had built were at risk. I was very disappointed and showed it.

After school, as I was sitting in the teacher's lounge deep in concentration, I did not notice him enter the room. Feeling a light tap on my shoulder, I looked up to see Brant. He appeared to be deeply distressed.

Lowering his head, Brant meekly eked out, "Darrell, it was me."

Before I could say a word, he went on. "I am sorry, and it will never happen again."

Catching eye contact and knowing that it is very hard for males to say, "I am sorry," I agonized over what to do.

"Brant, you put the entire program at risk," I calmly said.

At that point there was really nothing further to discuss. Holding eye contact, I simply said, "You will have to go to the bottom of the waiting list and earn your way back into the life sports program."

Observing his astonishment for not being emergency expelled on the spot, I explained to him, "If you had not said that you were sorry, like a man, I would have had to deal with you and you would not have liked it."

Letting the moment hang, I followed with, "You have shown great honor, see you tomorrow."

Brant nodded, turned politely, and left.

I let it go.

40. Camp Robbers

Sometimes, no matter how well I planned, things would still go wrong.

Several months after the Mount Si incident, I planned a snowshoeing trek for the platoon. On the way to Mount Rainier, we stopped at the Chevron convenience store in Eatonville. Having the Ohop Lake cabin, I spend time there during the summer buying groceries and gas for my boat. Knowing by sight, not by name, I oftentimes proudly shared with the store employees my goals regarding taking inner-city kids to the mountains on hikes and adventures.

While we were in the store, I monitored several platoon members as they traded off using the bathroom. As each person exited the bathroom, I would jokingly comment, "Did you wash?"

It's always surprised to catch so many that would forget to wash after doing their business. By their embarrassing expressions, they knew that they were supposed to have washed their hands. But, for some reason, they just didn't.

Not wanting any sticky fingers ruining my relationship with the store employees, I also watched closely as other platoon members grabbed some snacks and paid for them.

After leaving Eatonville, as usual, I stopped by the Alder Lake Dam and lectured about the Depression and Roosevelt's works program.

On ward, we drove on snow and ice for about ten miles after entering the national park. Once at the Longmire Inn, the yellow and red emergency hazard gate was blocking the entrance road to the Paradise Inn.

Puzzled, Parking next to the Longmire animal museum I told the platoon, "Go check out the indigenous animals while I locate a ranger."

Earl was the only one of the group to ask, "What is 'indigenous'?"

"Good question, 'Indigenous' means that they were always here, like the Native Americans." Earl was curious about things, and his mind seemed to always be working.

The Longmire museum had a fascinating display of stuffed animals and birds of the Pacific Northwest. Of course, it did not take long for platoon members to locate the bullet hole that had brought down the stuffed cougar. Guns and bullets always seemed to attract their attention. The museum provided us with a visual of the wildlife within the area.

Unable to locate a park ranger, I returned to the museum and took the platoon outside to try and figure out what to do.

Contemplating our options, I noticed that Earl, right out of his hand, was feeding some camp robbers. That was what I'd learned to call them anyway.

These particular gray and white birds had hit the jackpot. Earl was feeding them his entire school district baloney and cheese sandwich. Amazingly, Earl was acting just like a little kid. He was showing his million-dollar smile, amazed that the camp robbers would eat right out of his hand.

"Pearl, what are you doing?" I yelled out.

Angered by the interruption, Earl gave me a mad dog expression that said, "What do you think I am doing?"

190

Pausing from the feeding fest, Earl barked, "What did you call me?"

"What did I call him?" I thought.

"For some reason I called you 'Pearl!'" I shot back.

"Just leave me alone!" he responded to my interrupting his bonding moments with nature.

After several minutes, Earl approached me and abruptly asked, "What is the name of those birds?"

"We call them camp robbers."

"That can't be their name," said Earl with a tilt of his head.

Not very convincingly I said, "We call them camp robbers because they rob you of your food when you're not watching." I could tell by Earl's expression that the explanation was not good enough.

After a moment Earl asked, "Why did you call me Pearl?"

Distracted by a flying snowball flashing by my face, I directed my attention to the thrower. "You're damn lucky that didn't hit me or this would've been your last road trip!" I ripped out.

Without yelling, I firmly directed the throwers to go across the street to the Longmire nature trail for their snowball fight. That was the last snowball thrown in my direction.

Glancing back to finish the conversation with Pearl, he was gone. "What the heck?" I thought. "He knows the rules about never leaving the platoon without asking."

Worried, I checked the restroom, not there.

Several minutes later, from a distance, I spotted Pearl exiting the Longmire Inn with a park ranger. My first thoughts, of course, were, "What did he do now?"

Expecting the worst, Pearl came up to me with great excitement in his eyes and explained, "They're called gray jays."

"What?" I blasted, ready to unload on Pearl for breaking the rules.

Perplexed, with squinted eyes, I repeated myself, "What?"

"They're called gray jays!" Pearl repeated with pride.

"Wow, I did not know that. Thanks Pearl," sheepishly responding.

Looking at the ranger I asked, "I hope that he was not a bother."

Ranger Rick responded, "He's refreshing."

Watching Pearl quietly meander back across the snow-covered street to continue feeding the gray jays, I caught myself contemplating another lesson learned from a very inquisitive student.

Not listening I heard, "We will not be able to go snowshoeing at Paradise."

Breaking my concentration on Pearl, I noticed that Ranger Rick was watching the members of the platoon very closely after he spoke.

Observing his body language, I had to ask, "Is everything okay?"

Ranger Rick paused and calmly explained, "There are boulders covering the road to Paradise."

Pausing again for a second time and eyeing the platoon, he simply said, "I can still take you snowshoeing, if you want to go."

"That's an easy one—let's go," I excitedly responded.

"Okay, everyone, get to the back of the van," I yelled out.

Distributing my personal snow gear to the unprepared platoon members, I noticed under the back seat a torn garden glove's price tag from the Eatonville corner store. Standing near the cashier's counter, next to the bathroom door, I did not recall anyone buying gloves and became quite suspicious.

Reaching in to pick the price tag up, tucking it into my back pocket, I slyly glanced around to see who was wearing a pair of new garden gloves. Wearing my blue parka and tan leather ski hat, I noticed that James Pierce was wearing a pair of thin brown garden gloves.

I thought, "This is not the time for confrontation." To be honest, I was not sure what to do.

As we were strapping on our snow shoes, it was impressive to see platoon members assisting each other. In the mountains, gang ranks were dropped and Region 5 students seemed to be more their inner core selves. In the woods, we were a platoon of guys out on another adventure, not gangsters, burglars, sex offenders, or murderers.

With everyone almost strapped in, I explained the ground rules: "Follow the Boy Scout buddy system, stay together, and do not lose me."

Ranger Rick gave a demonstration on snowshoe trekking and explained, "It is easy to trip if you walk on each other's snowshoes." He also talked about hyperthermia. "If you're unprotected, your body temperature can drop to dangerous levels in a matter of minutes."

While Ranger Rick was speaking, impressive was watching Juan helping another Hispanic student get strapped into his snowshoes—leadership is learned.

I also noticed that Brant was roaming through the group double-checking that everyone had a hat and gloves. With everyone taken care of, without a hat, he asked me, "Are there any hats left?"

Smiling with pride at his display of leadership, I gave him the hat off my head and told him, "I have my hair and beard to keep me warm."

Watching Brant put my hat on reminded me of something, and I asked the group, "Why do you want to cover your head?"

No one responded, so I went on to explain, "You can lose eighty percent of your body heat through your head."

"Where is *your* hat?" someone popped off.

I mockingly said, "Listen, tough guys, I care for you so much, I'd give my life and my hat for you."

Waiting for a response that did not develop, I let it hang. I broke the silence by adding, "That's why you guys are wearing all of my snow gear—I do not want anyone to get lost and freeze to death out here."

The platoon gave me a courtesy laugh, but I was serious. I had a flashback of the Hilltop Crips getting lost hiking down from Lake

George. That had been a close call, and it was still fresh in my memory.

After posing for a group picture we began our single-file snow-shoeing trek through the thick Douglas fir forest. After about a half mile of trekking, concerned, I noticed that there was no trail for us to follow. It appeared that Ranger Rick was forging the trail as we went.

Though alarmed at first, this snowshoeing trek turned out to be the most beautiful snowshoeing experience that I have ever had. I was used to going on the same route to the Nisqually glacier, taking a few pictures along the way, and hiking back. Snowshoeing through untouched snow was remarkable. We went around trees, up and down hills, and through the woods as if we were on heavenly clouds.

At one point, so mesmerized by the experience, I almost didn't notice that Juan and his buddy slipped behind us for a smoke.

Getting a weird feeling, my Guardian Angel's presence emerged and luckily, I glanced back over my right shoulder.

Taking several steps back toward Juan I said, "We had better not lose Ranger Rick."

Juan just looked at me trustingly and said, "You know where were we are going."

In as serious a voice as I could muster without alarming them, I confessed, "Juan, I have no idea where we are."

Pausing to check the seriousness of my expression, Juan just looked at me. Then, to save them for later, he and his buddy quickly snuffed out their cigarettes with their fingertips. Almost as a reflex, they secured the butts into their coat pockets.

After their cigarette remnant saving ritual, we wasted little time hooking back up with the rest of the platoon.

Once we broke through the thick snow-covered forest, Ranger Rick had guided us to the Nisqually River. Spending a lot of time in the forest hiking, I was surprised to be completely turned around.

Spreading out from our single-file march like a platoon on a military patrol in Russian Siberia, I noticed Brant standing by himself near the river looking up at something. Approaching, I asked, "What are you looking at?"

Brant simply replied, "Look at that."

Looking up the river basin, Brant was right—the view was spectacular. As we were looking at Mount Rainier, I yelled to everyone, "Stop, hey, take a look!"

In a moment of silence, we were caught in awe by the overpowering immense beauty of the snow-covered mountain. Glancing at Pearl; he seemed stunned by the panoramic view.

If not for Brant, we would have missed it.

Tearing my eyes away from Mount Rainier, I noticed that James was standing with his arms out and his palms down waving them back and forth in a circular motion. Snowshoeing up to him, I asked, "Did you see how beautiful Mount Rainier is?"

Ignoring my question, James just looked down and around at all the snow and said, "This is just like cocaine."

"Pierce, cocaine is not what I expect you to be thinking about on road trips."

Looking at the stolen brown garden gloves I went on to explain, "Nature and drugs do not mix!" Not happy about the theft from my favorite Eatonville corner store, shaking my head, I snowshoed away.

After snowshoeing along the Nisqually River for about a mile, Ranger Rick motioned to a slight hill. Climbing up, he turned to help the next guy and then disappeared into the forest without saying a word. To my surprise, the first snow trekker that was helped to the top of the slight hill, turned and helped the next guy. And so it went, each platoon member helping the other up the slight hill and then followed Ranger Rick's single narrow path back into the dense forest.

Impressive, without verbal instruction, in single file, they helped each other up the slippery snow-covered hill. They were working together as a team. Watching, I was amazed to see blue and red guys helping each other. It was one of those teaching moments that I will always remember.

After cresting the slight hill from the snow-covered Nisqually River, we ended up right back where we had started, the Longmire Museum. Ranger Rick had taken us on a five-mile circular trek, and we did not even know it.

After we removed our snowshoes, I caught Ranger Rick observing the platoon with a curious look on his face. Getting his attention, I blabbered, "I had no idea where we were going."

Ignoring my comment, Ranger Rick looked at me and said, "I had a good feeling about this group."

In my teacher voice I asked, "What do you mean?"

Looking back at the group helping each other take their snowshoes off and stacking them near the building as they had been instructed, he said, "I got the feeling that these guys had community."

41. Brown Gloves

After snowshoeing and before we left the Longmire Inn rest area, policing up around the van I happened to look down and notice a pair of soaking wet wadded-up brown garden gloves. The gloves were haphazardly tossed under the right rear tire next to the sliding door of the van.

Without a word to Brant, who was helping me pack the wet snow gear into the rear of the van, I scooped up the gloves without anyone noticing.

Several miles down the road, as we were leaving the Mount Rainier National Park, glancing back, I made eye contact with James. Pulling the wet brown garden gloves from my coat pocket, I placed them on the middle console for everyone to see.

Brant looked down and asked, "Where did those come from?"

While steering with one hand, reaching into my right back pocket, pulling out the torn price tag I showed it to Brant. He just looked at me and shook his head in disgust, "What are you going to do?"

Making quick eye contact with Brant and looking back down the highway I simply responded, "I am not sure."

Several minutes later as we were almost at Alder Lake, I was not surprised to see that almost everyone was asleep. The five-mile snowshoeing trek had been a taxing experience. Noticing that

James was awake, I wondered if he had noticed the brown gloves on the middle console between the driver and passenger bucket seats.

Loud enough for anyone who might be awake in the van to hear, I asked Brant, "Do you want to know why I never steal?"

Brant did not utter a word, and I could tell that he knew what was coming next. "When I was about six years old, my mother bought me a plastic car model kit and a tube of glue for my birthday. My mother was a single parent with four kids and could not afford the paint to go with it."

Making momentary eye contact with James, I continued, "One afternoon, when she was away at work, walking to the local grocery store, I stole several small jars of paint."

Pausing, wanting James' attention, I went on. "Weird, I specifically remember one bottle was metallic blue. Oh yeah, in addition to stealing several small bottles of paint, I also stole several brushes. I was very proud of my completed car model."

Talking loud enough for others to hear, I continued, "When my mom got home from work, I showed her my metallic blue handbrushed painted car model with great pride."

Smiling, she asked, 'Where did you get the paint?'"

Taking a breath, looking in the rearview mirror, I could see that James was still awake and refused to look in my direction.

"At six years old thinking that I was smarter than my mom, I told her that the paints had come with the model. I thought the issue was over and went about admiring my car model."

Loudly I continuing my story, "Within an hour there was a knock on our front door and my mom, who was pretending to be busy, asked me to get it. Opening the door, I looked up to see, in full uniform, my mother's good friend Tacoma police officer Grin Legge."

Making brief eye contact with James, I continued, "Being about six foot tall, Officer Legge looked down at me and said, 'Where did the paints came from?'"

Frozen, I uttered out, "Lucky's."

Pausing for the effect, I continued, "Towering over me, Officer Legge calmly said, 'Let's take a ride.'"

Trying to make brief eye contact through the rearview mirror, I noticed that James appeared to be listening as he stared out the van window.

"I remember being placed in the back of the patrol car and noticing that the door handles had been removed. Officer Legge did not say a word. I was petrified."

"With the siren blazing, we drove directly to Lucky's Grocery Store from where I had stolen the small jars of paints. Escorting me to the manager's office, I was horrified to be taken back to the scene of the crime."

Pausing for a longer than normal period, I noticed that James looked in my direction seeming to anticipate the ending of my story.

"Once in the manager's office, and being scared to death, Officer Legge asked me if there was anything that I wanted to say. I do not remember what I said. I don't even remember the manager's face. I do remember the feeling of fear that I was going to jail."

Trying to gain eye contact with James, I continued, "For punishment, I had to work the price of the paints off by doing chores for my mom."

Again, I let the story hang for a few minutes trying to catch eye contact with James. Refusing to turn his head and engage me, I assumed that he had gotten my message.

Upon entering Eatonville, I did not pull into the convenience store parking lot. Parking on the street would give James and me a chance to talk before we entered the store.

As most of the students were waking up someone asked, "Can we catch a smoke?" In a stern, not mean voice I replied, "James and I have some business to take care of and I would appreciate it if everyone stayed in the van."

Picking up the half-dried brown garden gloves and the price tag, I motioned James to come with me. James had a deer-in-the-head-lights expression on his face and shook his head from side to side.

With anger building I calmly said, "James, you will come with me right now or I will drive you directly to the police station! Is that what you want?"

As the van windows began to fog, it was a standoff. I'm not sure if I would have taken him to the Eatonville police station or not. I knew from experience, you did not make a threat, unless you were ready to carry it out. As I waited, the van was deafeningly quiet.

"It's your choice. You decide, right now!" I said in a raised voice, taking my stand.

James, who was a Hilltop Crip, shot me an evil look.

"James, you have nowhere else to go, and you are going to face up to this!" I said more calmly.

After James fumbled over several bodies on his way out of the van and stood before me, there was an eerie quietness that sur-rounded us. It reminded me of animals and birds vanishing before an impending disaster.

As we proceeded to the store, James was walking about a half step behind me. Turning, looking him calmly in the eyes, I said, "There is nowhere to run—look around. Where are you going to go?"

James, giving me a mad dog look, said nothing.

"We are going to face this like men. I am with you on this."

Forcing eye contact, I calmly stated, "You have humiliated the African-American community..."

"What are you talking about!" James angrily blurted out.

Feeling eyes upon us, while trying to maintain eye contact with him, I went on to explain, "How many African-Americans do you think these guys see? Now, because of you, every time they see an African-American they are going to think that he is a thief! Do you understand the impression that your actions have left?"

Looking at James to see if he was connecting the dots, I went on. "If anything, we are going to show these guys that African-Americans have the honor to fess up when they make mistakes."

Squared up, man to man, I continued, "You are going to go in that store and apologize for stealing. You will also tell them that you will not do it again."

James with an expression of anger blurted out, "I don't have any money to pay for the gloves!"

"James, relax. If you show these guys honor, I will pay for the gloves."

As we entered the Eatonville convenience store, there were three male clerks behind the counter. I felt lucky recognizing two of men from stopping there previously and felt confident that they would work with us in this situation.

Placing the damp gloves on the counter, looking at James, I simply asked, "James is there something that you would like to tell these gentlemen?"

"I stole these gloves because I didn't have any, I'm sorry."

The moment of silence that followed seemed unending until one of the clerks stepped forward and replied, "It takes a big man to confess and apologize."

As he spoke I could feel the presents of racial biases subsiding.

Sizing the two of us up, he went on to say, "If I had seen you steal the gloves, I would've called the police immediately. I made some mistakes as a kid, and I hope you'll learn from this."

Surprised that the clerk would share so much, I was expecting to use my charm to talk them out of calling the police. Instead, this was being handled in-house and what a relief. The clerk was turning the theft of a cheap pair of brown garden gloves into a lesson, not a punishment.

James looked down in what I hoped was shame and simply replied, "I'm sorry."

Not sure if James meant it or not, it sounded convincing. Before anyone changed their mind, glancing at James, I ushered him out of the convenience store with my eyes. He quietly eased himself out of the store and headed for the safety of the van.

Before making my exit, the clerk said, "You've stopped here on several occasions, and I've noticed that you travel with a rough-looking bunch."

Pausing for the right words, he concluded, "Spending time locked up, I was lucky to have learned my lessons at an early age. If I'd caught him stealing in the store, I would have called the police."

Glancing back at his buddies, hesitantly he looked down at the floor. Returning to the conversation, he finished the lesson with, "I'm impressed that you brought him back here to face the music."

Looking at the long-haired, tattooed, and bearded clerk, I was speechless. It was weird how my initial perceptions of him changed as he spoke. Through his actions, his image transformed from a tattooed leather-wearing biker to that of a normal good guy.

Glancing over at the other clerks and catching their expressions, I felt humiliated and proud at the same time. I do not remember paying for the gloves or just leaving them on the counter. Giving each of the clerks a firm handshake, I sincerely expressed, "I appreciate you working with me."

As with Police Officer Legge, James and I never spoke of the incident again. Hoping that the lesson was learned, why beat an issue into the ground by rehashing it?

James skipped the next several days of school, and I can only assume that he did so expecting to be suspended. Once he figured out that I did not notify his probation officer of the incident, he returned. I did not call his mother either regarding the theft. He had acted with honor, and the issue was over.

James was placed on the bottom of the life sports waiting list and unfortunately, did not show an interest in earning his way back into the program.

After that, while on road trips, I never stopped at a convenience store again.

42. Pearl

I t is interesting how perceptive the students at Region 5 were. They could almost sense that I was disappointed in James. For several days after our snowshoeing trek, they gave me a wide berth until I could sort things out.

In the beginning, I assumed that students would be everlastingly thankful for the things that I did for them. I was taught at an early age to be respectful and thankful to adults. It was impressed upon me by my parents that if you wanted someone to continue to be nice to you, you should be nice and thankful to them. Do unto others, as you would have them do unto you. Unfortunately, a lot of the students at Region 5 were not taught the same basic "Bible school" common sense courtesies that most of us learned at an early age.

Several days after the snowshoeing trek, while waiting for the group home van to pick him up, Earl took me aside and asked, "Why do you call me Pearl?"

Caught by surprise, in my teacher voice I popped off, "I challenge you to look it up in the dictionary and figure it out yourself."

Wrong answer, I could see the distressed expression on Pearl's face when he said, "I don't know how to use a dictionary."

Gently patting him on the shoulder to relieve the tension, I said, "I did not learn how to use a dictionary until I was in high school either. In fact, I did not start enjoying reading books cover to cover until I was twenty-two years old while fishing in Alaska."

With kindness I explained, "Earl, pearls come from salt water oysters. A pearl is formed when an unexpected particle like a speck of sand ends up inside the oyster as it grows."

"When I first met you, you were like a speck of sand. As I got to know you, I have watched you grow and develop similar to a pearl. Your layers shine. Your smile is an open invitation to conversation and your curiosity is refreshing. You have developed a positive glow about you."

Giving Pearl time to grasp what I was conveying, I continued. "Have you ever been in church and seen the glow around the minister as he speaks?"

Pearl did not respond.

Looking into Pearl's eyes, side-stepping that example, I explained, "You have taught me to never prejudge a person."

"You have proven to me that first impressions are not to be trusted. You have earned the name Pearl. You have a glow around you now."

Sensing that Pearl wanted to give me a hug, he did not make the move to do so.

Grabbing his right hand, pulling our clasped fists to our hearts, I wrapped my left arm around his right shoulder and gave him a firm man hug. After the brief embrace, the delight in his eyes and the huge smile on his face said it all.

Without a word, Pearl turned and walked away.

43. Broken Keys

S everal weeks after explaining to Earl the reason that he'd earned the nickname Pearl, he disappeared. Concerned, calling the group home to find his whereabouts, I was informed that Pearl had moved back home with his mother. I was disappointed that he'd moved back to Seattle without bothering to say goodbye.

Several days later, unexpectedly, Pearl showed up at the security door waiting to be checked in for school. Happy to see him, I almost hugged him as he passed through our medal detector. Concerned, I could not help but ask, "Where have you been?"

With a smile Earl explained, "My mother moved from Seattle to Tacoma for a fresh start."

Looking around to make sure that no one was listening he added, "I don't want anyone here to know where I live."

I whispered back, "That's a good idea, and a fresh start for your mom is great."

As days passed Pearl's attendance was sporadic. I was just glad that he was trying to attend. Generally when Region 5 students were no longer court connected, they disappear. He chose to attend even though he was not forced by the courts to do so.

One day while playing on the Word Grubber computer program, Pearl slammed his fists down on the keyboard so hard that individual keys went flying. With his head lowered he yelled, "I'm so stupid!"

The entire computer center went eerily dead quiet. Everyone knew that Pearl could become an intimidating person.

Walking over to Pearl, gently placing my hand on his shoulder, attempting to calm him down, I reassured him, "You have a lot to catch up on."

Pearl did not look up at me, but I could sense that he felt hopeless. "Pearl, what can I do to help?"

"If I had a computer, I would practice every day!"

Not knowing if I could loan a computer out or not I asked him, "If I set you up with a computer, would you really practice every day?" Pearl looked up at me and nodded.

It was perfect timing—we had just collected a dozen old surplus Apple IIe computers from one of the high schools. In addition, Brant was burning off community service hours helping me organize the garage into an Apple IIe assembly plant.

Initially, the plan was to use the computers for spare parts and for a small computer lab in my classroom. Pearl's frustration inspired me with the idea to place surplus computers in the homes of struggling Region 5 students.

That day, after school, guiding Pearl to the garage, Brant taught him how to piece together his own Apple IIe computer. In addition, we copied several of the skill building programs for him to take home, he was glowing with excitement.

After we loaded Pearl's computer into the van, we were on our way to his home.

Upon entering Pearl's apartment, it was shocking to see how little he and his mother had. There was a couch, a TV on a small stand, and a tiny dining room table with two chairs. There were no family photos on the walls or hanging pictures of any kind. I tried not to show my surprise.

After being introduced to Pearl's mother, sensing that she was surprised at who I was, she gave me the feeling that I was not the person she expected.

As we placed the computer parts on the dining room table, I continued to feel her eyes watching my every move.

Beaming with pride, Pearl demonstrated to his mother how to connect the simple components of the computer together. The old Apple IIe computer appeared to be the newest addition to their spartan apartment.

Almost in an embarrassing tone, Pearl's mother asked, "Is there any typing disks? Learning how to type would give me a better chance of getting a job."

Pausing to fully grasp what was happening, I assured her, "We have several typing disks at Region 5, I would be happy to make copies for you."

Her gratitude glowed from her expression. "Thank you."

Leaving Pearl's small Eastside apartment, I felt that we were giving them the needed tools to better themselves.

When working with court-connected students, we do not get to see a finished product. General education school teachers, those who participate, get graduation and other student accomplishments to validate their teaching or coaching abilities.

At Region 5 Learning Center, our hope was that our students would stay alive past their twenties.

What happened by dropping off the computer with Pearl and his mother is one of those "I did something right" moments that do not come along very often when working with street kids. It was an empowering feeling.

Computer recycling project helps students study at home

PEARL SELF-HELP TUTORIALS ASSIST STUDENTS WHO HAVE FALLEN BEHIND BY INSTALLING APPLE EQUIPMENT

BY DEBBY ABE   **NOVEMBER 3, 1999**

The News Tribune

A computer recycling project is proving how one person's junk can be another person's gold.

Teacher Darrell Hamlin and students at Region V Learning Center in Tacoma are collecting used Apple IIe computers to give to other center students.

The Apple IIe is an early 1980s-era computer considered ancient in a field that churns out faster and more powerful computers every few weeks. Most owners can't even give them away.

But Hamlin, lead teacher at Region V, uses the old workhorses to let his students practice their basic vocabulary, reading and arithmetic skills. And they need all the help they can get, he said.

Region V, funded by the Tacoma School District and Pierce County Juvenile Courts. Connected with Pierce County Juvenile Court, is intended to help young people convicted of crimes make the transition from juvenile institutions to regular schools. The students are 15 to 18 years old but often test at the fourth-or fifth-grade level, Hamlin said.

"We have found the basic skill level for students is so low we spend most of our time reteaching them," he said. "We're just trying to make a difference with a very needy population."

Their needs extend to many aspects of their lives.

Many have never seen a zoo, gone on a ferry ride or been to Mount Rainier until going on field trips in the program.

But some have seen parents killed, been abused themselves or try to commit suicide, Hamlin said. They may have committed theft, assault or even murder.

The idea is to put computers into his student's hands grew out of the frustrations of one student last year. In a fit of anger over his poor academic skills, the boy blurted out, "I am so stupid!"

Hamlin asked what he could do to help him learn. The boy, nicknamed Pearl, said, "If I had one of these computers at home, I'd work on it every day," Hamlin recalled.

The teacher arranged to install an Apple IIe with monitor, keyboard and educational software in the boy's apartment.

Hamlin and other students decided to try to do the same for other students, and christened their effort the Pearl Self Help Computer Tutorial Program.

They collected surplus computers, keyboards and monitors from the Tacoma School District, as well as donated sets. They make sure the computers work before giving them to Region V students. Since starting the program, they've placed more than 30 sets of computer hardware and software.

"Putting computers in their homes help them sharpen basic skills," Hamlin said.

Recipients and their parents sign a contract under which the student promises to work on the computer at least 30 minutes a day, five days a week. The computers are loaned to students, but they may keep them as long as they use them, Hamlin said.

Two Region V students living at the Carson Home in Fife last year were among those who received the computers.

Hamlin is asking for donations of Apple IIe computers so he can provide even more of them to his students.

"It's kind of empowering them to take accountability for their own acquisition of knowledge," Hamlin said. "That's what I like about it now. There's no more excuses."

After the article was published in *The News Tribune* the outpouring of contributions was overwhelming. I wish Pearl could have shared in the glory. Shortly after dropping the Apple IIe computer off, Pearl stopped attending school.

Typical—during the "Pearl Self Help Computer Program," I was asked several times by an administrator from Tacoma Central Schools for a list of student names regarding where the computers were placed.

After about the fourth or fifth time of asking and not receiving the requested information, I assume that he got the hint that there was no list.

To be honest, I did not intend to recollect the donated surplus computers that we placed into the student's homes. Some of the students shared with me that their siblings were using the computers too.

I was hoping that by not recollecting the out dated computers, entire families would be able to use them. As far as I was concerned, the computers were theirs to keep.

The program would not have been a success without Brant's help. After several months of keeping track of Brant's community service hours, I asked our secretary at the time, Alonda to calculate his time and write a letter for his probation officer.

Alonda was a perfect fit for Region 5. A single Hispanic mother with two daughters in college, being bilingual, she contributed greatly to working with our immerging Latino students. As with Leona, Alonda kept the learning center running smoothly.

Contacting Brant's probation officer, I was proud to inform him that Brant had accumulated a large amount of community service hours. I was surprised to find out that he had completed his community service hours months before.

Brant, not needing community service hours, had donated his free time after school to teach other students how to build their own Apple IIe computers.

I did not tell Brant that I had discovered his secret. I thought about Jake picking up the little girl by her feet, slapping her on the back, and popping the stuck piece of hot dog out of her throat. He had not expected recognition, and neither did Brant.

Until summer break, Brant continued to work building and placing computers in students' homes expecting nothing in return.

We ran the computer home tutorial program until we were bounced out of the Region 5 building to make room for the School of the Arts students.

After being displaced from Region 5 and locked out of the garage, I was informed that the remainder of our computer inventory had been taken to the Tacoma city dump.

What a shame.

44. Bus Stop

Waking early one Sunday morning, an odd flashback slipped into my thoughts. The vague dream was a reminder of a chance encounter with a former Region 5 student. For some reason, in the back of my subconscious, I had compartmentalized and forgotten about the reunion with him. As fast a dreams pass through the night, there are very few dream occurrences that I take the time to recall. This dream flashback was vividly fresh.

I was lying listening to the rain splatter onto the balcony outside my bedroom when his smile reappeared like the faded image of a dream.

Knowing that our girl's 10-and-under coach-pitch game would be rained out, relaxing, I could almost feel his gentle tap on my shoulder.

Along my journey to justify Region 5, I've written about the weird occurrences that have driven my quest. Articles dropping from books, lost diary writings, curled-up photos, and passing by certain areas of Tacoma have triggered submerged memories. I am embarrassed that this particular encounter was submerged for so long.

The chance encounter took place at the Remann Hall Day Reporting School bus stop. Not remembering the year it occurred and in the scheme of things, does the year even matter? Do to challenging work conditions, the many years of teaching in the criminal education system have been a blur to me anyway.

After a tough Monday of reminding students over and over again not to use the "F" word, I was worn out. Mondays are sometimes the worst days of the week. Students come back from their festive two-day break swearing and misbehaving more on Mondays than any other day of the week. We call it "Swearing Monday." By Wednesday, we usually have students back on track and using appropriate language.

Irritated and giving myself some space from the "swearers," I was standing alone while waiting for the Pierce Transit bus to pick up the students. It was not a good day, and I was having an adult time-out.

Mentally disconnected from the students, getting a weird feeling that someone was watching me, I instinctively glanced back and up the sidewalk toward the detention center. Near the entrance of the Day Reporting School and the halfway house for released adult ex-prisoners, I noticed three males meandering toward us. Three astride, one was walking in the street as they were talking and joking around.

Disgustingly I thought, "How typical—went to prison and cannot even follow a simple rule like walking on the sidewalk."

I looked away slightly shaking my head.

"Please don't use the 'F' word!" I barked off to one of the swearers.

Pausing to hold back my anger, I fired off without a smile, "Go to the TCC bus transfer station and swear!"

Frustrated with our students, magnetically, I was drawn back to the three ex-prisoners.

Closer now, noticing that the smiling street walker was the largest of the three men, I recall thinking, "How odd, even on the outs, he's still wearing the standard-issue matching prison clothing and shoes." The light tan durable loose-fitting pants and coat looked like a rough-cut knock-off of expensive carpentry work gear. The tan boots resembled a cheaper style of waffle-stomper boots that had been popular when I was in junior high school during the 1970s. Trying not to be noticed, turning my head, I thought, "I would not be caught dead in clothing like that!"

Lost in the moment, watching cars and trucks fly by, I felt a large, but gentle hand on my shoulder. Trying not to show it, I almost jumped out of my skin.

"Excuse me sir, did you teach at Region 5?"

Trying to relax, I was slow to respond, "Yes."

Casually squaring up to the man inside the faded tan prison garb, I noticed his smile first. Racing to remember, my brain was traveling too fast to place the name to the smile.

"Where is your beard?" he politely asked.

Puzzled, I jokingly gave my regular response to this question: "It was getting too gray. I'm not a grandfather yet."

While ignoring his friend's obvious distrust of me, he quietly asked, "Are you Darrell?"

As the pace of time slowed to a workable speed, I remembered, "Pearl!"

With his image visible in my mind, my entire outlook on that day changed from disgusted to joyful.

Grabbing his right hand with mine, pulling our joined fists to our hearts, I wrapped my left arm around his huge shoulder giving him a tight man hug.

I could see that Pearl's buddies were shocked by our embrace, glancing at them over Pearl's shoulder, they backed off.

As memories flooded my thoughts, Pearl was not anxious to break away.

Unwilling to release his hand, slightly stepping back, I commented with a grin, "Pearl, you look a little thicker than I remember."

"Prison food will do that to you," he said with his huge million-dollar smile.

"What happened to all your hair?" he teased back.

Feeling a negative presents of eyes upon us, ignoring it, I asked, "Are you here for very long?"

Locking eyes with me, Pearl bypassed my question with the tilt of his head. "I am never going back to prison again," he proclaimed glancing over at his buddies who had distanced themselves further away from us.

As time regained its normal speed, surprising both of us, the bus snuck up to disrupt our unplanned reunion.

Mumbling something to Pearl, his two buddies headed for the bus.

"Pearl, there is so much I would like to talk about." Knowing we had little time, I said to him, "I'll be here tomorrow!"

Not responding, Pearl shot me a huge smile.

Regaining my thoughts, and as if I could mentally remember, I asked, "What's your number?"

Making eye contact with his buddies as he walked toward the bus, Pearl did not respond. Slowly glancing back one more time, he gifted me a huge smile.

As he turned getting on the bus, I was overcome by a hollow feeling when he did not look back. Watching him walk the narrow aisle through the bus, window by window to be seated near his buddies, he did not glance out to give me a visual goodbye.

As the puff of diesel exhaust clouded the fading image of the bus, with a sad heart, I could not help but maintain a smile.

Many times over the next few weeks I would wait long after the bus had picked up the Day Reporting School students hoping to see Pearl.

I never saw Pearl again.

45. Dennis

Not exactly sure when it began, we started opening the computer center at Region 5 in the mornings for students who wanted to improve their basic skills.

After searching students for weapons and checking them for dress code violations, they could proceed to the computer center.

Working well for staff and students, they were supervised before the regular school day started and also could improve their basic skills by being on the computers. Students could play Gambling Man, Word Grubber, or practice the spelling computer disks.

Generally, I took the lead in supervising the computer center before school. On this particular morning, I had to excuse myself for a few minutes to use the bathroom. The men's bathroom was directly across from the computer center, and I was close enough to hear through the door if there was a disruption.

Seated peacefully on the toilet doing my business, all of a sudden a huge commotion erupted in the computer center. From my position, I heard what sounded like chairs being pushed around and a scream. Scrambling, I barely got the door opened to see skinny Tubes Baker bolt from the computer center holding his nose with blood seeping through his fingers.

Living at the group home, Tubes Baker was a harmless student who took advantage of the extra computer time every morning.

His real name was Charles Prince. He earned the nickname Tubes Baker while inner-tubing. Several times a year I would take students up to Mount Rainier National Park's Paradise Inn for an inner-tubing excursion.

Tubes Baker was king of the hill.

In regard to inner-tubing, upon arrival at the historic Paradise Inn, we would go sliding on gigantic black semi truck inner tubes down a snow-covered hill at warp speeds. We collected the inner tubes from the Goodyear truck stop on Puyallup Avenue near Fife, Washington. Larry, the manager, through the years was more than happy to provide us with used patched semi truck inner tubes to use for tubing.

In preparation for tubing, we would haul the deflated inner tubes to the small town of Elbe, fill a dozen or more up, tie them to the top of our sixteen-passenger van, and drive up to the Paradise Inn to inner tube on the snow.

For safety purposes, the Mount Rainier rangers would gouge out a hundred-yard downhill snow track for people to safely inner tube, or so they thought. With Tubes Baker's guidance, the platoon slightly modified the course to create added thrills.

While on probation, Tubes Baker lived in a group home taking every opportunity to go on Region 5 road trips.

While inner-tubing, Tubes patiently taught other platoon members how to make inner-tubing trains. By linking our arms and legs together, with our combined weight for momentum, just like a train, we would fly down the hill in single file eight to ten tube riders in a row.

Thrilling also was stacking riders in pyramid style—eight people high and racing down the snow covered hill. Now that was a wild ride!

Tubes Baker was "the man" when it came to inner-tubing. Toward the end of the day, on that particular road trip, he and several other students built a jump at the end of the tubing ramp.

If the park rangers had been supervising at the time, they would never have allowed it.

Often after being airborne, students would be thrown from the bouncing inner tube ending up in a huge human dog pile, a mass of legs and arms.

In addition to being very exciting, it was great exercise. Carrying our inflated tubes, we had to hike up the snow-covered hill to be able to rocket back down at maximum speeds.

Tubing is a great inexpensive activity for students who had never been inner-tubing on snow before. It was a healthy activity that we wanted our students to one day share with their children. In fact, several times through the years at Region 5, we would give parents who asked inner tubes to take for their families. It was rewarding helping families get excited about healthy outdoor activities.

Rare for Region 5, Tubes Baker was a gentle and kind guy. Staying to himself, he did not cause anyone grief. Measured from the top of his short brown curly hair, he was about five foot four and barely weighed 110 pounds. Witnessing him dashing from the computer center grasping his nose with blood seeping out between his fingers was a startling surprise.

Upon entering the computer center, in confusion, I saw several students yelling at a guy that I did not recognize.

Centering himself in the middle of the computer center, fists clenched, he was ready to continue the fight.

Looking at the assaulter and never taking my eyes off of him, firmly, I asked anyone that was offering, "What happened to Tubes Baker?"

Several students pointed to what appeared to be a crazy blue-eyed maniac and shot back in unison, "He started it!"

Seeing that the suspect's eyes were wide with rage and his long curly blonde hair was askew as if he had just gotten out of bed, I was concerned form our safety.

Continuing to try and make eye contact with the assaulter, I ordered everyone else out of the computer center.

Positioning myself at the door, I blocked the aggressor from leaving. We did not have a security guard, never did, so to resolve situations, it was up to staff to creatively dissolve potentially dangerous situations.

In as calm a voice as I could muster, I asked, "Who are you?"

Appearing half crazed and emanating evil, looking at me with glossed-over eyes, he demanded, "Just who the hell are you?"

In a more stern voice, I explained, "I am the lead teacher in this building. If you cause me any grief, I will call the police and press formal assault charges against you!"

Pausing to wait for a reaction that did not materialize, I shot a command, "Now sit down! Sit down now!"

We were at a standoff—neither was going to budge. As several other staff entered the computer center, Crazy Blue Eyes made the right decision and had a seat.

Within thirty minutes, the emergency expulsion paperwork was done and Crazy Blue Eye's parents and probation officer were notified.

In some cases when parole students were being disruptive, I would drive them directly to the Juvenile Rehabilitation Administration Building. Located up the street from Region 5, just past the Hilltop war zone, it was located on 19th and Sprague Street. Word spread quickly through the student grapevine that those who were driven to the JRA building would receive severe consequences from their parole officers.

In this situation, Crazy Blue Eyes was a court connected student from Remann Hall Detention Center. Using the school van, I decided to drive him home myself. Driving suspended students home was a tactic that I used as lead teacher to defuse situations. While driving disruptive students home, as a captive audience, I would explain what they had done wrong and re-establish clear expectations of future behaviors.

This was one of those times.

Driving without making eye contact with Crazy Blue Eyes, I explained, "It is not okay to assault people, and if you ever do that again I'll call the police myself to have you arrested."

Several times Crazy Blue Eyes tried to interrupt me with excuses and I had to shout him down, repeating, "You just close your mouth and listen!"

"I missed your enrollment, and if I had done your enrollment, I would have made it clear to you that assaulting people is wrong!"

Finally getting silence, I explained in a harsh tone, "We do not settle things at Region 5 by fighting."

Mumbling out the directions to his house, I noticed that the route we were taking was one of the alternating routes that I took to work and drove home. The closer we got to my house, becoming concerned, I thought, "What a freak coincidence it would be if this crazy guy was my neighbor?"

As we pulled up to Crazy Blue Eyes' house, looking at the side of his head, feeling evil emanating from his soul, I said, "You better get your act together or you will not be attending Region 5."

Slowly turning his head, expressionless, looking through me he said, "There's nowhere else for me to go!"

As he was leaving the van, getting his attention one more time, I said, "If you mess with me, I'll make your life very uncomfortable."

Seeing him look away, I added, "If, we allow you to attend Region 5, you better make a complete change in your behaviors!"

As he exited, the slamming of the door made the van tremble slightly.

At that point, I was mad enough to jump out of the van and confront him again, man to man. Trying to remain calm, I decided to let it go. Having an uneasy feeling about this guy, I had a suspicion that he was bad news to the core.

Once back at the building, covering my class, I relieved Katie our paraprofessional at the time.

Katie and I usually played good cop bad cop with volatile students to defuse dangerous situations. The Crazy Blue Eyes incident erupted too quickly and violently to implement our strategy.

Katie had a sixth sense in regard to developing hostile situations. Many times with a light pat on the shoulder and calming advice; she could bring everyone, including me, back to our senses.

Looking back, it is remarkable the unique people that passed through Region 5 who tried to make a difference with a very tough group of kids. Katie exemplified the unique personalities and gifts staff were trying to bestow upon the students.

Wow, what a way to start the day.

As we were eating lunch with the students, I casually took the opportunity to ask several students what had happened. In light conversation and while eating, students will generally share more details. Several angry students informed me that Tubes Baker and Crazy Blue Eyes were arguing over a computer. After listening to several students, turning, I asked Roman, "Who did the enrollment for this crazy blue-eyed nut?"

Roman, taking a defensive tone, said, "Well, I did the enrollment."

"Was there any indication to you that this guy was unstable?"

Roman did not mess around during enrollments—he was a perfectionist. Looking at me, he said, "I had no idea that young man was volatile."

"Roman, I'm not blaming you, I'm just shocked that this happened so early in the morning on his first day."

Embarrassed, I whispered, "I was on the toilet doing my business when it happened, and didn't even have a chance to wipe and wash."

Pausing, we both chuckled.

Changing the subject, I asked, "Did you have a chance to talk to the group home about Tubes Baker's injuries?"

"The group home thought that Charles's nose might be broken."

"I can't believe that crazy blue-eyed psycho broke Tube Baker's nose. All this happened because Tubes would not give him the computer that he was using," I added with a grunt of disgust.

Before leaving school that day, I called the group home to find out how Tubes Baker was doing. It was true—Crazy Blue Eyes had broken Tubes Baker's nose. My feeling of anger for the defenseless Tubes Baker was at its peak.

Hoping, I asked, "Is Charles going to press charges?"

The group home response did not surprise me. "No, he just wants to do his time and go home."

Tubes Baker did not deserve to get slugged in the face over a dumb computer.

46. Fresh Start

When a student is suspended or expelled from Region 5 Learning Center, we would have a reentry meeting in the round room with the student's parents and probation officer. More times than not, the P.O. was generally the only one in attendance. Several days after the Tubes Baker's assault, we scheduled Crazy Blue Eyes' reentry meeting for after school and made it mandatory that his parents be in attendance.

On the day of the scheduled meeting, entering the building after life sports, I was surprised to see Crazy Blue Eyes, his parents, and his probation officer there early. Crazy Blue Eyes and his parents were closely scrutinizing the many field trip photo-poster boards mounted on the Region 5 interior walls.

Once everyone was in the round room, Roman took the lead. Pulling out Crazy Blue Eyes' behavior and dress code contracts, he clarified that he had in fact signed both agreements. Roman was diplomatic when he reviewed each requirement one by one, again. This was not a reflection upon him, but he was going to make clear that if Crazy Blue Eyes deviated from the contract again, he would be out.

Picking up where Roman left off, I explained to Crazy Blue Eyes, "Your behaviors were out of control, and it will not be tolerated here." With Tubes Baker on my mind, I tried to speak calmly.

Being stern, I added, "I have no idea who you are, what your record is, or where you come from, and I really don't care. You get a fresh start here, a fresh start that you may not get anywhere else in Tacoma Schools."

Letting my comments hang, my younger brother Johnny popped into my thoughts. After being bounced from one school to another, he eventually gave up and dropped out of high school at an early age.

Regrouping my thoughts, I went on, "How many of us can get a fresh start? Not too many people do, but here, you get one and you're just about to blow it!"

Gently interrupting, his mother pleaded, "There is no other school that will take him. This is his last chance."

Looking around the group with a sorrowful expression, she turned to me and said, "We hope that you will give him another try?"

Pausing to think things through, I noticed his mother was wearing a wedding ring and assumed that unlike most of the Region 5 students, his parents were still married. Feeling the anguish and frustration emanating from her, I recall that his Crazy Blue Eye's father did not speak at all.

Breaking eye contact with his mother, I looked back at their son; he again reminded me of my brother. He certainly acted like him. As my mind was racing, I thought back to the problems that my brother had caused our family. I recall asking myself a question "Was the school system partially to blame?" "Did Johnny ever get a clean slate?"

Weird, Crazy Blue Eyes even looked like my brother. They both had blond hair, about six foot-two, strong, and had anger problems. My brother went out of control at about the age of thirteen and was rarely held accountable for his behavior and as a consequence, still isn't.

Pondering their similarities, I noticed that the room was eerily quiet. Breaking the encompassing silence, looking at Crazy Blue Eyes I asked, "Well, what do you have to say for yourself?"

After making brief eye contact, Dennis—his real name—looked down and simply said, "Sometimes I have no idea why I do the things I do."

I felt like asking, "Are you insane?" But being a professional, biting my tongue, I held my true thoughts to myself.

Dennis' probation officer asked if he could speak in private to him and his parents. As we stepped out, the door began to vibrate in unison with the re-addressing of Crazy Blue Eye's current behaviors. Speechlessly listening through the closed door, we could hear the probation officer unloading.

Unnoticed, we slipped away from the area to the safety of our staff lounge.

Dennis had a strong support system and a tough probation officer. We were not too sure how this was going to turn out, but we decided to give him a fresh slate.

47. My Bad

One thing I found interesting, intriguing even, at Region 5 Learning Center, was that situations evolved as destiny in motion.

I did not anticipate a violent confrontation between Crazy Blue Eyes and Tubes Baker. When they did see each other again, I planned to stand back and observe from a safe listening distance as their interactions unfolded. I was confident that Tubes Baker was not a vengeful person. How could a guy with a twenty-four/seven smile like his, be mean?

Tubes Baker was a happy young man and was just counting the "wake-ups" until he was free of the juvenile justice system and could go home. I have no idea what crime he committed, and give his behaviors at Region 5, I did not care.

When Tubes Baker and Crazy Blue Eyes met again, within hearing distance, I saw Crazy Blue Eyes reach out his hand and say, "I am sorry."

He did not say, "My bad" like the rest of the tough guys. He actually said, "I am sorry." Very impressed, I thought, "Maybe there is hope for this guy after all."

Pausing for a moment to size Crazy Blue Eyes up, tilting his head and smiling, Tubes held out his hand and simply said, "Nice to meet you. My name is Charles Prince."

That handshake sealed a relationship that developed into a solid friendship.

48. Braggart

Unfortunately, Crazy Blue Eyes was suspended on several more occasions. His inter-personal communication skills were horrible. His behaviors were like grinding fingernails on a slate chalk board—he rubbed most people the wrong way.

The weird thing was, Blue Eyes did not understand why students always wanted to fight him. I spent most of my time defusing potential fights that he would get himself into. Constantly saying weird things to other students, their reaction was to want to punch him out.

Unintentionally provoking, in addition to saying weird offensive comments, Blue Eyes continually told other students huge fictitious stories about himself. My guess was that he told embellished stories to try and make friends.

I often recall telling him, "You do not have to tell stories to make friends—we already like you."

After a while, that particular statement was ineffective, so every time Blue Eyes would start a tall tale, I would bluntly interrupt him and say, "You do not have to lie to make friends!"

Eventually, he began to keep his behaviors in check and the endless tall tales faded away. We were all thankful.

49. Lost Bus Pass

I do not know how it got started, but driving Blue Eyes home every day was like volunteering to do something on the job. At first, you volunteer to do something from the kindness of your heart. Unfortunately sometimes, that which you volunteer for today becomes part of your job and is expected.

One day after school, about a mile away from Region 5 Learning Center near Wright Park, I noticed Blue Eyes walking home instead of taking the bus. Wright Park is located between downtown Tacoma and what is called Old Town Tacoma. The beautifully wooded city park area with crushed gravel walking paths is also adjacent to the Hilltop area. Being a beautiful inner-city park during the day, it was a scary place at night.

Pulling over, from my car window, I asked, "Why aren't you taking the bus?"

Barely looking at me, Blue Eyes angrily blurted out, "I lost my bus pass, and that 'old hag' of a secretary won't give me another one!"

"Hey, wait a minute!" I said. "Besides you being rude to her on a daily basis, we only have so much money for bus passes and the funds come right out of our budget."

Pausing to double check to see if he was listening, I further explained, "If someone loses their bus pass, it is not our responsibility to replace it."

Blue Eyes just looked at me and without saying a word turned and walked away. Feeling a little sympathetic, I drove up next to him and reluctantly said, "Hop in. I'll give you a ride."

As we drove toward his house, I took the opportunity, being that he was a captive audience, to explain some common sense perceptions. "Look, it is nothing personal, me being tough on you." Without making eye contact I told him, "You attract a lot of negative attention."

Softly I went on. "If I ignored your weird behaviors, you would be under the impression that they were acceptable." Not trying to hurt his feelings, I continued, "Everyone knows that most of the stories coming out of your mouth are made up."

Staring out the windshield in an almost trance like state, Blue Eyes asked, "Darrell, do you believe in God?"

As my thoughts slammed to a halt, I instinctively replied, "Yes."

As the silence grew, I added, "A man is not judged by the Bible he carries or the gold cross worn around his neck."

"A good man is judged by his actions, good or bad."

Blue Eyes didn't say a word, and as if ignoring me, he turned and asked, "When can I be in to PE? When can I go on the life sports field trips?"

Ignoring the question, pulling in front of his house, I tried to get him to look me in the eyes. Unsuccessful, I simply stated, "Until your behaviors improve, you will never be in life sports!"

Before leaving my car, I asked him, "Are you a good guy or a bad guy?"

"Are you on the dark side or the good side, evil or just, what is its!"

Getting out of my car, not the van, he did not slam the door as usual.

Seeming not happy with my response, never looking back, he stomped off like a little kid with a bruised ego.

Weird, Blue Eyes waited for me almost every day for a ride home. It was on my way, so I did not mind. I did take the opportunity to address his weird behaviorism of the day and made suggestions on how to act more appropriately.

On one occasion while driving him home, I had to ask, "How did you end up at Region 5?"

Looking straight ahead, in a justified tone, Blue Eyes said, "They should never have left their keys in the car with it running."

50. Inner Course

Blue Eyes eventually worked his way into the life sports program. Still a rascal at school, he was one of those disruptive students who attended every single day. It was almost as if he had nothing better to do.

I am not going to lie about it. There are some students when greeting them at the door, I think to myself, "Could you at least skip one day now and then to give us a break?" But, being a professional, I greet every student, every day with a warm welcome.

On one occasion, as with many, during life sports Blue Eyes was complaining about something. If it wasn't a headache, it was a stomach ache or some other ailment. I had never known a person with so many excuses for nonperformance. Time and time again I made it clear to him, "The goal is to run a mile nonstop. If you cannot do it, then you cannot be in life sports."

One afternoon when we were going to run our mile on the inside trail at Point Defiance Park, renamed the "inner course" by the platoon. As usual, Blue Eyes had a number of excuses as to why he could not run a mile nonstop. Tired of the daily battery of excuses, I finally told him, "If you do not run a mile nonstop today, you're out!"

Not interested in his response, turning, I started jogging down the trail.

The inner course mile run started at the furthest point of the Five Mile Drive at Point Defiance Park. The walking trail itself divides the park in half. We would start our run at the Gig Harbor viewpoint overlooking the Narrows channel. Most of the platoon members knew that Point Defiance was named by Captain Charles Wilkes. In 1841, exploring for the United States, Wilkes proclaimed to the world that from the Point Defiance vantage point, with cannons, he could defy the world. The image stuck and the park was eventually named Point Defiance.

Often, the lead runners at the half mile point would turn around and as we passed slower runners would encourage them to keep going. Passing Blue Eyes, I noticed that he was limping and blurted out, "Stop faking, just finish the mile!"

"I think, I think I broke my ankle," Blue Eyes exclaimed in a whimper.

Stopping to set Blue Eyes straight, I said, "Listen, every single day it is one excuse after another. I am sick and tired of your excuses. Just finish the mile or you are out!" Turning, I jogged off.

Waiting longer than anticipated for Blue Eyes at the end of the run, as usual he was the last to finish. Shaking my head in disgust I simply said, "You can stop with the act. At least you tried."

"I broke my ankle," Blue Eyes proclaimed to no one listening.

Pausing, administering a look of disappointment, I said, "Fine, you don't have to play pickle ball today. Is that what you want?" Limping over to the van, he got in without saying a word.

The next morning, exiting the staff lounge with a cup of coffee, I noticed Blue Eyes being helped out of his parents' car with crutches. My first thought was, "He is taking this faked broken ankle a little too far." Then I noticed that his foot was encased in a white plaster cast.

Watching in despair, my heart sank to the deepest pit of my soul, and I thought, "I am going to get a butt chewing for this one."

Surprisingly, Blue Eye's parents did not enter the building. Setting off the metal detector with his crutches, with the hugest smile that I have ever seen, he burst out, "I wasn't lying. I told you I broke my ankle."

Stunned, "Dennis, I am so sorry," was about all I could say.

Still smiling, Dennis asked, "Does this mean that I am kicked out of PE?"

"No, I guess this means that you get to ride in the front seat."

The front passenger seat is generally reserved for the student who has been in the life sports program the longest. It is odd, but riding in the front seat was a major accomplishment for platoon members. The person who rode in the front passenger seat was generally given more responsibilities and took on a leadership role with the platoon. When Dennis hobbled into the front seat with his crutches and cast that day, there were no objections from other platoon members. Running the inner course with a broken ankle was one of the toughest tests of courage that a platoon member had ever accomplished. After that day, Dennis had earned the respect of every platoon member.

Returning back to Region 5 after life sports, I anticipated a major reprimand from our principal Mack. I remember visualizing Mack rubbing his bald head in disgust trying to figure how to deal with me. Forcing a student to run a mile with a broken ankle could be interpreted as negligence.

As I sat waiting, the infamous words of Margaret also kept repeating their haunting warning: "If you break the law, you're on your own."

Luckily for me that day, I did not have to drive Dennis home. When Dennis's parents came and picked him up after school, so embarrassed, I did not even go out and talk to them. I was certain that the life sports program was in jeopardy, maybe even my job.

Sulking around feeling sorry for myself, anticipating the dreaded administrative visit, Roman came into my classroom and in his diplomatic manner simply said, "What is the most that they can do to you?"

Letting it hang with no response, I just shrugged.

"Roman, you know as well as I do, one negative erases a hundred positives."

Roman as usual was very supportive and replied, "Who else could they get to do this job?"

As the days passed I came to realize that Dennis's parents did not file a formal complaint about the incident. I was shocked; if my son had come home and told me that his teacher forced him to run a mile on a broken ankle, I would have gone ballistic. I would have called every administrator possible and possibly *The News Tribune.* This was another lesson for me, no matter how many precautions teachers and administrators take, sometimes things just happen.

Dennis showed great honor by taking responsibility for breaking his ankle. This was the first time that he did not blame someone else. Realistically, who else was there to blame, the tree root that he tripped over?

Before his broken ankle, Dennis blamed everyone else for almost everything he did. Could an exposed tree root on a trail at Point Defiance Park have taught him the lesson that we were all trying to teach? As weird as it may sound, a large exposed tree root taught Dennis that he was responsible for his own actions.

As time passed, Dennis' only major concern was that he would not be able to go on the upcoming snow inner tubing road trip. I assured him that we would postpone it until his cast was removed.

That was all he wanted to hear.

51. Twelve Weeks

To Dennis the twelve weeks in a cast must have passed very slowly. To me, in the context of time, it was just a blink. At Region 5 Learning Center there were so many daily conflicts to defuse, that time passed very quickly.

True to my word, we waited to do our final inner-tubing trip of the year until Dennis could go.

The excitement emanating from Dennis was enough to drive everyone crazy. His day had come, and between him and Tubes Baker, the energy level was high.

On the day of our long-awaited departure, Dennis came early to help load the inner tubes into the van. Once at the Elbe store and gas station, he managed the process of filling the inner tubes with air. In addition, he and Tubes Baker were more than happy to help tie the huge semi-truck inner tubes to the top of the van.

Knowing the impatient anticipation, we bypassed the Longmire Wild Animal Museum and headed directly to the historic Paradise Inn Lodge. With the inviting energy of a sunny day, as expected, the park rangers had gouged out a perfect inner tubing course for us to speed down.

To increase the speed, Dennis had brought with him an added tubing advantage. Smiling from ear to ear, he pulled out of his backpack a large piece of wax. Wasting little time and not asking permission, he started waxing the under surface of the tubes. Tubes Baker was more than happy to assist.

We had an excellent day with not a cloud in the sky. In addition, platoon members were having a great time and getting along well.

As usual, directed by Tubes Baker, we created the longest inner tubing train in Mount Rainier history. Hooked by our arms and legs, our eyes watered as we raced down the steep snow slicked course. With the added wax, it felt as if our giant black inner-tubes were flying on top of the snow.

To add to the excitement, Tubes Baker and Dennis came up with the idea to have two jumps, in a row, at the bottom of the tubing course. Not anticipating the ramifications, reluctantly, I gave the go-ahead nod.

The two snow jumps at the bottom of the inner-tube course had to be the wildest ride most of the platoon members would ever take. Stacked in a pyramid six to eight people high on the inner-tube, traveling quickly out of control, the first jump took out two or three riders who tumbled off laughing. Those who miraculously hung on were tossed off by the next jump. Undeterred, the platoon members continued to fly down, crash, and burn for the rest of the day.

Was it dangerous? Yes, maybe, but so was living on the Hilltop or Eastside of Tacoma.

During our tubing frenzy, toward the end of the day, we had drawn a crowd of onlookers. Watching their expressions, they reminded me of the type of "lookie- loos" you see slowing down after a car accident on the freeway. They had the gaze of people wishing to leave, but were uncontrollably drawn to the next crash.

Trying to leave at about 3:30 p.m. to make the long drive home was quite the task. How do you break the news to young teenagers who are having the time of their lives that the party is over?

As usual, we ended up giving half of our inner tubes to families who had come unprepared. I was confident that Larry at the

Goodyear truck stop would be more than happy to replenish the inner tubes that we shared with others. The gift of giving is taught—we are not born with it.

The drive down the mountain was long and quiet. Before we hit Longmire everyone was fast asleep. This had been an excellent outing, one that Dennis well deserved.

To reinforce the leadership qualities that Dennis had developed, I put him and Tubes Baker in charge of creating the inner-tubing road trip photo-poster board. Giving them time from class, I set them loose on their own in the lunchroom to cut and paste to their delight.

In addition, as usual, I had an 8×10 group picture made, framed and ready to be delivered to Larry at the Goodyear truck stop. I thought it would be appropriate for Tubes Baker and Dennis to deliver the framed photo themselves. I wanted Larry to know first-hand what a positive impact he had made on Region 5 students.

Both Tubes and Dennis were very thankful and grateful when they delivered the photo to Larry. Of course, afterwards, I treated us to hot fudge sundaes.

By the end of the year most students would be leaving Region 5 and not returning. Tubes Baker had returned to Bellingham and Dennis was excited to get a fresh start at a traditional high school.

As with most students when they left, we generally did not hear from them again. Dennis was an exception. He called several times the following year, and one day he very excitedly informed us that he had made the high school wrestling team and had joined the student Junior Reserve Officers Training Corp, the JROTC. Encouraging, I told him, "Discipline and structure is the way to success."

During his senior year at his high school, Dennis was chosen as the most improved student and was interviewed by *The News Tribune.*

Against all odds, many will still graduate

BY JAMI LEABOW FARKAS   JUNE 2, 1993

The News Tribune

Catherine Jones said she never thought the day would come that she would see her son, Dennis, in a graduation cap and gown.

A Pierce County Jail jumpsuit would be more like it, she thought.

In and out of trouble with the law during middle school and in his early high school years, Dennis Jones was one kid probably few people thought would succeed.

But on Monday, Dennis will be among the 270 Stadium High School students who will march into the Tacoma Dome as seniors and march out as high school graduates.

It's a sight those who know Dennis thought they might never see.

Dennis Jones never had it easy in school. From the fourth grade on, he was put into special classes because of a condition known as attention deficit hyperactivity disorder. It makes it difficult to control his impulses or anger, he said.

By the time he reached middle school, he was mixed with students who were bad influences, he said. He shoplifted and stole small items like portable stereos. He was booked into Remann Hall on suspension of taking a motor vehicle while a freshman at Wilson High School, he said.

He was sent to Region V Learning Center in Tacoma, attended by students on parole or probation or expelled from school. On his second day there, he got into a fight and broke the nose of his opponent, he said.

Jones eventually returned to Wilson and got into trouble yet again, and was sent back to Region V, where he rekindled

246

a friendship with teacher Darrell Hamlin. With the support of Hamlin, his parents and long time doctor, Dennis said he came to a realization.

"Things started changing inside of me," said Dennis, 17. "I wanted life other than in the juvenile justice system."

And he was willing to work for it.

At Region V, he worked with Hamlin, who became his trusted teacher. He toiled in summer school to make up lost credits. He eventually enrolled at Stadium this year.

His hard work paid off. He will graduate in the standard four years with a grade-point average of 2.61 on a scale of 4.0, up from a 0.65 he had in his early high school years.

He also fulfilled a longtime goal this year by competing on Stadium's wrestling team and has spent the current semester at Bates Technical College studying auto-body repair, the field in which he is looking for a job.

"I really enjoyed this year. I wish it could have always been like this," he said. "It's been a long, hard road."

Hamlin and Jones' mother said Jones, the graduate, is a young man far removed from Jones, the juvenile offended.

"He was out of control. I didn't even want him in my (physical education) program," Hamlin said. "We hit heads so much it was incredible."

Now, Hamlin said, Jones has made "a total turn around. He's probably the most improved human being I know."

Catherine Jones agreed. She, her husband and their 19-year-old daughter, likely are to be among the proudest people at Stadium' ceremonies.

"I'll probably cry. I was really afraid what his future was going to be," Catherine Jones said, "If he can graduate, any of them can graduate."

52. Identity

When Tacoma School District decided to move Region 5 Learning Center to another location, I was displaced from my position. I put up an unsuccessful battle against the Tacoma School Board of Directors to leave Region 5 at its current location.

As my battle raged, locating former Region 5 students and their parents to speak on behalf of our learning center to the school board was a difficult task.

Struggling, I asked Dennis' mother for help, she was more than happy to send a letter on our behalf. Her correspondence was directed to the superintendant of public instruction and to the members of the Tacoma School Board. She addressed the issue regarding moving Region 5 students to portable buildings in an isolated area of the Oakland Alternative High School campus.

To whom it may concern,

Our son, Dennis Jones attended Region 5 in 1991-92. Dennis was severely attention deficit hyperactive disorder. He began running into problems with the law when he started shop lifting at age 9. By age 16, he stole two cars, spent time in Remann Hall and then was sent to Region 5. At Region 5, he found teachers who were willing to work with less than perfect students, teachers who took the time to explain things to students who had trouble learning, who didn't learn the same way other student do. For the first time, he was in a school where kids like him weren't known by the rest of the school as the "bad kids" or the "troubled kids." They were just kids. Most importantly of all for Dennis, he met Darrell Hamlin. Darrell took a personal interest in all of "his kids. He befriended them, he taught them social skills as well as academic skills, he played ball with them and he disciplined them. Darrell looked upon these kids as valuable people, people who could change and who could contribute positively to society despite their early mistakes and the kids knew he saw them this way. Dennis took that faith that Darrell placed in him and turned his life around. By the time Dennis graduated from high school he had been voted the "turn-around" student of the year. Dennis deserves a huge amount of the credit for these changes, but so do the staff and program at Region 5 Learning Center. He and Darrell kept in contact along time after Dennis left Region 5. Darrell would call and check up on Dennis, encourage him, and let him know that he hadn't been forgotten. This made a huge impact in Dennis' perception of himself and of life. Someone cared about him who didn't "have to"—like parents have to. He was valued for who he was, a person.

These kids have been in trouble, many are likely to get in trouble again. But for all of them, a sense of identity is important. Some will get that identity from gangs or by being identified as bad. Region 5 works to give these kids a positive sense of identity to replace the one they came to the school with. Having their own school not only keeps others safe from any dangerous acts these kids might commit, but it also gives these kids a place where they can grow, learn and develop positive skills for life. The teachers who staff this school are unique; they really love and value these kids and that is not a characteristic that can be taught or mandated. Kids recognize true concern. Darrell and the other teachers at Region 5 have given these kids what Tacoma schools system failed to give them earlier in their learning career – a place to belong, to be valued, to call their own. These kids still need that place. They need to know that their education matters as much as it does for any other kids in the school district. Being moved out of their school and into portables, segregated from other kids at the school sends a message to these kids that they really aren't worth as much as the other kids. It returns them to the identity as the "bad kids." This is definitely not a sigh of progress.

Please reconsider this move. As a parent, we will be grateful forever for what Region 5 did for our son. Please allow it to continue to work it's healing and teaching on other kids.

Sincerely,

Catherine Jones

53. Step-Students

I worked for fifteen years in the Hilltop area of Tacoma at Region 5 Learning Center before the program was moved to another location. Region 5 was perfectly located to create a neutral place for different gang members and court-connected students to attend school and feel safe. At 19th and Tacoma Avenue South, we were a school with our own identity for the students that other schools did not want—we created a community.

The program move is a long story. The short version is, all the Region 5 staff were displaced by an angry administrator and not rehired after interviews.

As sad as it sounds, our court-connected voiceless "step-students" of the district were bounced out of their school to make room for the Tacoma School of the Arts students.

Fighting with passion to have the wheels of destruction reversed, in the end, they rolled over us. We were left lying in the ditch like road kill on a distant mountain highway.

The type of students we worked with had little value to Tacoma Schools. Street kids brought down the district test scores and as a result, were left out of the educational system to fend for themselves. "No Child Left Behind" should be changed to "Leave the Lower Test Scoring Students Behind."

Region 5 students also lacked the type of parents who were sophisticated enough to work the system. The new location of Region 5 was a disaster, and the program eventually closed.

54. Jackey

The other day, eight years after the destruction of Region 5, I got up at about 7:30 a.m. from our mountain cabin located in Packwood, Washington, and headed up to White Pass ski resort to cleanse my thoughts. My aim was to do some solo downhill snow skiing and relax.

Working with court-connected students for as long as I have, I am a more patient teacher after a fun weekend activity. Many times, a walk on the beach, a bike ride, or just hanging out at the old Ohop Lake cabin can be enough to rejuvenate me for the following week.

White Pass ski resort is located eastbound from Interstate 5 along Highway 12 en route to Yakima. The state patrol refers to Highway 12 as the "Heroin Highway" of Washington State. More black tar heroin is transported along Highway 12 from Yakima to Interstate 5 than on any other highway in the state. Trying to nab drug runners, the Washington State Patrol uses probable cause justifications to pull over as many cars as possible. More convicted felons are caught through traffic violation than any other method. In fact, the capture of Tacoma's evil mass murder Ted Bundy was captured during a routine traffic stop.

On Highway 12, I try to do the speed limit and not attract attention to my driving.

My children both had sleep-over birthday parties at friends' houses Saturday night, so I had taken the opportunity to head up to the mountain by myself. Unfortunately, skiing conditions were poor; there was light rain and the snow was slushy. Happy Drake and Kaylee were not with me, these types of skiing conditions are miserable with kids.

Loading onto chairlift #6, getting comfortable, a solo snowboarder recklessly raced up to barely load onto the chair with me. Appearing to be your average teenage skateboarder turned snowboarder, his boarding gear was mismatched and he was not wearing any protective head gear.

Upon closer examination, from under his stocking cap, I noticed some type of electrical wires hanging down from his covered ears. The thin wires were neatly slipped inside his beat-up dirty parka.

Riding the chairlift by myself most of the day as a result of the unfavorable skiing conditions, I welcomed the chance for some conversation. To break the ice, I asked Board-Head the typical chairlift question: "Where are you from?"

Barely glancing over toward me, as if he could barely hear, in a louder than normal voice, he replied, "Packwood."

Surprised, I responded, "Our family has a cabin in High Valley."- For some reason, I did not feel comfortable enough to tell him the location.

Almost not listening, in a half-raised voice he went on to tell me, "Yesterday was a horrible rainy day at the Pass!" Surprisingly, he added, "Today is a much better day for cruising in and out of the trees!"

Soaked to the bone and skiing on slushy snow. I thought to myself, "This guy must be stoned!"

Listening to him talk, he appeared to be a typical teenager, a little wacky and free-spirited. Then I asked, "Do you know a girl named Jackey Johnson?"

Pausing to pull out the wires that were attached to his hidden ears, with a bit of a smirk, he leisurely commented, "Yeah, I turned her."

Shocked, I quickly responded, "Turned her!"

Glancing away as the trees beneath us whipped by, I recall thinking to myself, "Jackey is a prostitute?" I had heard the term "turned her" used many times from Region 5 students.

Repeating Board-Head's offhanded comment in my thoughts, instantly I felt a pain in my heart and flashed back to Ellen who'd worn the fluffy pink sweater. To think that Jackey had gone to the dark side deeply saddened me. Then a thought emerged. "I've never heard of prostitution in Packwood." Doing my teacher thing, I asked, "What do you mean 'turned her?'"

Board-Head looked at me as if I were simple in the head and said with pride, "I got her onto the stuff."

Remembering that Jackey was charged with possession of a controlled substance, I just had to ask, "Why did you do that?"

Looking at me as if I were not listening, he boasted, "We were all doing it."

At that moment, I saw Board-Head's actions for what they really were, evil.

When Jackey first arrived at the Remann Hall Day Reporting School, I noticed that she rarely spoke. When she did, she would cover her mouth. To get her to speak at all was quite the task. The other girls at school thought that she was snotty and stuck up. As a result, I was continually defusing potential fights between her and the other girls.

One day while talking to Jackey, being relaxed, she forgot to cover her mouth.

Noticing my shocked expression, with a reddening face, she quickly covered the scars. Her brownish teeth were in stark contrast to her persona. Jackey was an attractive fifteen-year-old young lady, very intelligent and well spoken. When she opened her mouth, the horror of her addiction was clearly evident. She used methamphetamines, and her teeth were the gruesome after-effects.

As I thought about Jackey and Board-Head who'd practically bragged about getting her hooked on meth, from my new point of view, his entire appearance changed. Looking at his scraggly facial hair, raggedy clothes, and mis-matched gloves, I felt like throwing him off the chairlift into the passing trees below.

The memories of so many impressionable Region 5 students raced through my mind. McFly, Crispus, Jessica, and PJ, to name a few popped into my thoughts like emerging gray jays from a dense forest. Through the years, I have seen so many lost souls that could have been saved. To this day, while pondering the different students whom I have worked with, a dark shadow of sadness overcomes me.

What Board-Head did to Jackey was evil. He might as well have had horns and a tail.

Suppressing the urge to stab him with my ski pole, I asked him, "Where is Jackey now?"

I was praying that Board-Head was going to tell me that she was off the meth and had her life back together. "I really liked Jackey, she was very smart and an excellent student," I added, hoping for the best.

Board-Head flatly responded, "She is married and is still on the stuff with her husband." With a smirk that said, please punch me in the face, he slipped in, "I'm not on that anymore."

I wanted to scream in his face, "Sure, you slowly drag a nice young thirteen-year-old girl into the evil world of methamphetamines, and then you bail out!"

Board-Head must have sensed my anger building and muffled out, "It's her mother's fault. You should see how whacked out she is."

Looking through Board-Head, not really listening to his babble, I was questioning whether I should have even asked about her at all. When Jackey left the Day Reporting School, I was sure that she would make it. She had everything going for her. She could read, write, and had a great personality. All that slowly lost to methamphetamines.

Years later, after Region 5, Jackey was no different than the others, a victim of evil that had slowly stolen her soul like the eroding waters of a river. Similar to most of the other students whom I have worked with, she had been overcome by the dark side.

Of all the people that I had to ride the chairlift with it had to be Board-Head the punk. He cast further ruin onto my already rainy Sunday solo snow skiing day.

Losing concentration, I spent the rest of my day haphazardly skiing in the slush and muck. Events and student's faces were emerging like ghosts wanting their voices to be heard. I asked myself several times, "Why are these coincidences continually happening?"

To make matters worse, in my excitement to ski by myself, I had packed lightly and not for skiing in the rain. Searching for clothing in my bag, the only clean dry clothes were my black and gold Star Trek pajamas.

"Great, what if the state patrol pulls me over wearing these?" I said out loud to no one but myself.

The long nonstop drive home from White Pass to Tacoma was no different. In silence, wearing my "Trek" pajamas, sipping hot tea with the window down to keep me awake, I could not escape the haunting memories of Region 5 students. Pearl, Clark, Smiley, and others kept surfacing.

Unable to silence their images, I tried listening to music to squash the memories. Not helping, their images kept emerging like eerie ghostly shadows trying to be seen.

The same question went round and round in my thoughts: "Where are they now?"

55. The Gaggle

everal weeks after the Jackey Board-Head incident, driving home on the Mountain Highway from White Pass, passing an isolated convenience store, an unexpected heartwarming memory broke free. The vision of our random encounter brought a smile to my face.

Several years earlier, driving home from a ski trip at White Pass with my children, tired, I pulled into the same isolated convenience store. Often flying past, the small gas station store is near the Roy Y turn-off, down the street from Pacific Avenue in Spanaway.

Having an empty parking lot to choose from, without thinking, for some reason I was drawn right next to a blue minivan.

Drake, my son, as usual was fast asleep, but Kaylee, always awake and alert, wanted a snack. Getting sleepy, I needed some hot tea to keep me awake for the last leg of our trip.

Glancing across to the blue minivan as I put back on my left shoe, I observed four or five young kids unbuckled and bouncing around from seat to seat. The van was dirty and the windows were fogging up as a result of their uncontrolled activity. I could tell that their mother was struggling to keep everyone seated and in line. Not trying to stare, she appeared to be frazzled. "Who wouldn't be?" I thought without saying. All on her own, she reminded me of a typical single Tacoma mother with a gaggle of kids.

Leading the way into the store, Kaylee disappeared around the corner of the shelved products. Entering in her dust, without seeing her, I shot a verbal reminder, "We are not buying any candy or pop!"

"Yeeesss, Dad", I heard from behind the shelves of goodies. We had recently set the goal that on road trips candy and pop were out.

On a quest for hot orange spice tea and heading toward the coffee section at the rear of the store, I noticed that the mother entered the small store and was glancing around. It was relief to see that her gaggle of rascals had remained in the minivan.

Unable to release my gaze as she stood at the front door, she appeared to be disorientated and worn out. From across the store, I could almost see the dark shadows under her eyes. Her hair was askew and she looked pale. "No make-up needed tonight," I thought sarcastically.

Still caught by her appearance and unable to pull my eyes away, I was actually looking through her to another time in my life. Upon closer observation, she reminded me of how tired my mother had looked when I was a kid. Without conscious thought, I began to recall how tough it had been for my mother. Being a single mother with four kids, my mother wore the same exhausted expression after working long hours at the Winthrop Hotel in downtown Tacoma.

Reflecting back upon my childhood, evil always seemed to be knocking at our front door, my mother being the defender. In a haze, I thought to myself, "Was this familiar woman also the defender of her family?"

Returning back to normal time, I refocused my gaze upon her. For some reason, she seemed familiar. Not knowing why, I felt like we had met before, instinctively I knew our paths had crossed. When our eyes met from a distance, noticing a slight smile appear on her face, I was caught wondering, "Does she recognize me?"

It was one of those "got-you" moments where you are caught staring at someone, and when they look at you, you quickly try to turn away without being noticed. As if magnetized, I could not break my stare.

In what seemed like an instant, walking over, she gave me a gentle hug.

Surprised, I thought, "Now the pressure is on." I had to know her, but could not place a name to the warm smile.

Breaking the long embrace, she said, "I did not recognize you at first without your beard." Lightly touching the back of my head she said, "You're wearing your hair a lot shorter too."

As she spoke, tilted her head slightly, and leisurely brushed her long brown hair aside, I recognized exactly who she was, Deanna.

"Deanna," I said. "How have you been?"

Immediately I sensed by her evolving emotions that she was comforted by the fact that I remembered her name.

"How long had it been?" I thought. "In man time, it could have been five, ten, or fifteen years?"

"Did it matter?" I pondered.

Looking at Deanna, she appeared to be older than her age. Thinking without saying, "Thirty-two, maybe?" Parenting will do that to you and I had to ask, "Are all of those kids yours?"

With another tilt of her head, she smiled. "I have three kids. The other two I'm watching for a friend. Do you remember Angel?" Not waiting for my reply she went on. "They are her kids."

Typical, I thought, "She was always the mother hen of the platoon too."

In what seemed like an instant, Kaylee appeared with a bag of chips and water. Deanna glanced down and said, "This must be your daughter. She seems to be about the same age as my oldest."

In what appeared to be an afterthought, Deanna looked at me and slyly whispered, "I figured you to be a bachelor for life." Taking her attention from me, she asked Kaylee, "How old are you?" After small talk with Kaylee, she redirected her attention back toward me, "Kaylee is very polite and respectful."

Deanna's words barely registered. I was lost in thought as our Region 5 road trip adventures started emerging from my memories.

As we continued to visit, I could not help but reflect upon one of the scariest road trips that we had ever taken. Interrupting the flow of conversation, I blurted out, "Do you remember the rock?"

With a reddening face and a serious expression, Deanna broke eye contact, looked back down at Kaylee, and proudly proclaimed, "Your daddy saved my life."

56. Guardian Angel

When I first started working with court-connected youth it was rare that we had female students in attendance. Toward the end of my fifteen-year career at Region 5, the student population was generally seventy-five percent boys and twenty-five percent girls.

Most of the court-connected girls enrolled at Region 5 were rough. They had to be to end up at Region 5 and survive. Deanna was different. She had a soft side to her and was the motherly type. I do not mean to say that she would not "puff up" to defend herself, but she had a kindness and a glow about her that other students did not emanate.

While at Region 5, we did hundreds of life sports road trips. Unfortunately, as a result of insurance liabilities, the Day Reporting School where I teach now will not support such activities. For that matter, most people today would probably not take the same risks. Now, having a family of my own, I am not sure that I would either.

It is odd to say, but sometimes, when everything seemed to be going out of control, I never felt alone.

Reflecting back on the adventures that we shared, I always had the feeling that a Guardian Angel was looking over us. On several occasions I have tried to figure out who my guardian angel could be. My instincts tell me that it is my grandfather Herb Packard. He spent a lot of time with me as a kid and I took care of him until the day he died. My grandfather was not a church going guy, but he followed the basic Bible teachings. He taught me life-building skills; a strong work ethic, always tell the truth, and believe in family. At times, I can almost feel his presence.

In regard to Deanna's comment to Kaylee about saving her life, our guardian angel was with us that frightening day.

Our test of faith occurred during the a spring semester. I do not remember the year, but as a result of Deanna and Angel's continued protests, we planned a road trip that included several of the girls. Deanna and Angel were adamant that they could do anything that the boys could do. Adhering to their appeals, having little choice, I picked the date for the field trip and left it up to them to decide which one.

Honestly, I did not feel comfortable taking girls on road trips. Not that I anticipated that they were not strong enough for it. My mother and two older sisters proved to me at an early age that there is no difference between girls and boys except for societal expectations placed upon them. I just felt more protective of the girls than the boys.

Scanning the road trip photo-poster boards that covered almost every inch of the interior halls of Region 5, for their road trip, Deanna and Angel picked the snowshoeing expedition at the Paradise Inn on Mount Rainier.

Several days later, early one morning, we were on our way.

As usual, en route via the Mountain Highway to the Mount Rainier National Park, we stopped at the Alder Lake Dam which was followed by my standard lecture of the Great Depression emphasizing how President Roosevelt's works program saved America.

Passing under the mammoth cedar log arch that was the entrance to the national park, surprising, the park rangers' pay booths were empty. Finding it odd, we continued toward our destination.

As we passed by the left-hand turn-off to the Westside Road, one of the students toward the back of the van pointed to it with excitement. With pride, he began sharing with anyone that would listen about his adventures to Lake George. I thought to myself, "There are lots of festive stories on this mountain."

As we approached the Longmire Inn area and the animal museum, noticing a slight rain pushing against the windshield, I silently contemplated the snow conditions. Veering slightly left as we passed the ancient Longmire Inn, I was surprised to see that the yellow and orange emergency gate was blocking our path.

Caught off guard, we were left thirty miles away from the historic Paradise Inn. Not wanting to alarm the platoon, I quickly swung right into the Longmire Animal Museum parking lot. I assumed that the platoon would be able to tour the museum while I tried to locate a ranger, unfortunately the museum door was also locked.

As we were standing around like lost out-of-state tourists, a female park ranger emerged from somewhere out of the thick evergreen forest. I recall getting a weird feeling that she had been watching us the entire time.

Looking stern and matter of fact, she informed us, "An avalanche of snow has covered the road to the Paradise Inn." Appearing to be at a loss for words, she made no further comment.

"We are here to go snowshoeing. We are from Tacoma Schools and—"

Cutting me off, Ms. Ranger said, "There will be no snowshoeing today. The road is closed."

By the expressions on our faces, unless she was simple in the head, she had to have seen our disappointment.

Standing in a rigid posture, wearing a wrinkle-free spotless green uniform, I sensed that Ms. Ranger was not at ease. Feeling obligated to the platoon, I had to at least ask, "Are there any snowshoes available for us here?"

As she scanned the group, her flat-line emotionless response was, "All of our snowshoes are stored at the Paradise Inn."

Pausing to make sure she was watching, in an exaggerated motion, I glanced toward the park administrative offices across the street. I wanted her know that I was aware of the snowshoes stored there. From past expeditions, I knew that there were snowshoes available right across the street, she knew it too.

Her eyes gave it away; she was uncomfortable. Scanning the platoon, frustrated, I did not understand her misgivings.

Bringing my attention back toward Ms. Ranger and knowing that my nonverbal gestures toward the park offices were ignored, I had to make a decision. The silence that began to encompass us was eerie. Peering back into Ms. Ranger's eyes and then glancing at the platoon, I decided to let it go and head for home.

Loaded up and heading out, the feeling of despair surrounded all of us.

"What do we do now?" someone asked from the back of the van.

After pausing to suppress my frustration, I threw out, "Has anyone heard of Boxcar Canyon?"

From the very back seat of the van, hidden, a recognizable voice echoed out, "Yeah, we used to catch a buzz and jump from the cliffs next to the train tracks."

"Thanks, but you could have left out the buzzed part!" I responded. Peering through the rearview mirror, barely able to see his red hair and freckled face, making eye contact with Red, I fired back, "You better watch your comments!"

After making sure he was paying attention, I let him have it, "You're lucky to be on this trip after that episode with your brother last semester!"

57. Red Cadillac

Red was the younger brother to one of the original Caucasian Eastside Bloods who had attended Region 5. When the Crips and Bloods originally expanded their drug distribution operations up the West Coast I-5 corridor from Los Angeles, they were a racially segregated organization. Being an African-Americans-only club, they also distinctly adhered to different gang territories in Tacoma. The Bloods were on the Eastside, and the Crips dominated the Hilltop area.

In regard to their territories, on several occasions after a road trip, while driving the blue maxi van on the Eastside, I was concerned about getting shot at while dropping students off. The urban legend was that anything blue on the Eastside or red on the Hill Top was fair game for destruction.

An example of the personal impact of gang territorial rituals was when my former wife drove a red Pontiac Sunbird. Two months in a row, on the twenty-third of the month, her driver's side window was shot out. Complaining to another staff member during lunch about the insurance co-pay deductible expenditures that we had to pay, one of the Hilltop Crips took me aside and privately explained, "After our meetings on the twenty-third of every month, we go out and attack anything that is red."

Surprised, I was disappointed in myself for not figuring that one out on my own. From that point forward, on the twenty-third of every month, by parking our red car in the backyard it was the last time that our car's windows were shot out.

Red, I assumed by his curly red hair and freckles, was from Irish descent. He was not a cold-hearted guy. Sadly, he was greatly influenced by his older brother who claimed to be an Eastside Blood. Red's brother was tight with a huge muscular Samoan who was also a Blood. They had spent some time in the Region 5 life sports program, so I'd had an opportunity to build a relationship with the both of them. Unfortunately, they did not attend regularly and were mean and confrontational individuals.

Red's brother and the Samoan were an example of the gangs in Tacoma evolving from being strictly a segregated African-American organization to a multicultural one. It is believe that the Eastside Bloods desegregated their ranks to expand their drug distribution network into the white middle-class neighborhoods of Tacoma. As time passed, the 23rd Street Hilltop Crips also began to fracture into smaller multicultural organizations.

The previous semester, Red had instigated a gang fight several blocks away from the Region 5 building. On that particular occasion, we had three new wanna-be Hilltop Crip gang members trying to claim rank at Region 5. The three of them and Red were trying to establish a new power pecking order. Similar to most of our students who got involved in gangs, they were young, about thirteen or fourteen years old.

Red was not a tough guy, if not for his older brother, he would have stayed clear of gang activity. Generally, he was a nice guy.

After exchanging a few threats between themselves, the wanna-be Crips and the charlatan Red were sternly counseled. In addition, they were threatened with an emergency expulsion if the hostilities were not squashed. After our warning, we were confident that the conflict was over. Not the case.

After lunch, before we left for our life sports activities, noticing that Red was using the round room telephone unsupervised, confronting him, I demanded, "Who are you talking to?" Hanging up the phone, wickedly smiling, he brushed by me and walked off.

Immediately I informed Roman of the developing situation. Being second in command, he was in charge when I was out of the building. Expressing with concern, I said, "My gut tells me something is going down."

Ready for action, after life sports I parked the van directly in front of the Region 5 building front door and stood my ground.

As school was letting out Roman followed the students onto the sidewalk and cautiously asked, "Why did you park the van in front of the building?"

I quietly confided, "I have a bad feeling, and want to be ready to respond quickly if anything erupts."

While talking to Roman, I observed that after exiting the building the three young Crips and Red were silently walking in opposite directions. Red walked across South 19th Street and headed toward the bus stop. Watching him, I noticed that he slithered past the bus stop and was standing on the other side of the pharmaceutical building. Trying to be sneaky, Red was hiding half in and half out of the parking lot continuing to watch the Crips from what he thought was a hidden vantage point.

Taking my eyes off of Red, looking around, I noticed that the Crips were turning left and walking up South 18th Street toward St. Joseph's Hospital. I do not know how to explain it, but that little voice, my Guardian Angel's, was getting louder and louder: "Be careful!"

Keeping an eye on Red as a Pierce Transit bus passed, noticing that he did not get on the bus; I observed that he was still partially visible and appeared to be trying to hide.

Looking in his direction, several blocks away, I noticed an old 1970s series red four-door Cadillac with a white top approaching.

Stopping twenty yards from the stoplight, Red dart across the street and hopped into the back seat. Pausing for a few seconds, the Cadillac blazed through the red light with no regard to cross traffic.

As the Cadillac flashed by us, I noticed Red's brother in the passenger seat and his buddy the big Samoan driving. Never turning to look in our direction, they raced by us before turning abruptly left up 18th Street in the same direction as the wanna-be Crips had gone. As a reflex, I turned to Roman, "Call the police and tell them there is a gang fight and guns are involved!"

"Guns? Are you sure?" replied Roman in confusion.

"I don't care what you tell them! Tell them there's a fire!" Trying to remain calm for Roman's sake, I confided, "I have a bad feeling about this my friend."

Jumping into the van, not reentering the street, I drove half on the sidewalk and half on the grass the remainder of the block. Barely swerving around a cement electrical pole, I gunned it.

Flying off the curb, I cut a quick left and pushed the accelerator pedal completely to the floor. Cresting the hill almost airborne, noticing the red Cadillac to my right, I observed the big Samoan opening the rear trunk and reaching in to grab something.

Hitting the brakes and sliding sideways, the smoke from the screeching tires partially obscured the Samoan. Slamming the van into the parking gear, with the motor running, I jumped from the van like a wild man leaving the driver's side door wide open.

Halting the beating that they were giving to the younger Hilltop Crips, the adult Eastside Bloods were startled by the screeching tires and smoke.

With burning tire rubber filling my nostrils, I cleared the smoke and approached the gang. I left enough distance between us so that if they bum rushed me, I would still have enough time to hop into the van and run them down. I recall seriously thinking to myself, "If they come after me, I will run right over them!"

Pointing to each one the Blood gang members simultaneously, yelling almost at the top of my lungs, I said, "I know every single one of you!" Pausing, I fired off, "I will testify against you in court if you don't get your butts out of here!"

Captivated by the evil essence that followed, the tense silence was eerily spooky. As if breaking a spell, our standoff was interrupted by a distant echo of hollering.

Glancing slightly left, from across an open overgrown grassy field, above the remains of a fragmented cement foundation; I faintly connected the hollering to an African American women waving about recklessly. Perched on the balcony of an apartment complex, her raised voice captivated everyone's attention.

Trying not to take my eyes off of the gangsters, I observed a purple bathrobe with two arms swinging around like sticks pointing and shaking in the wind. From the narrow balcony, she was repeatedly hollering, "I called the police and they're on their way!"

Breaking into my fight or flight mentality, from behind me, hearing huffing and puffing, I knew without looking that it was Roman. Wearing a dress suit, he wore one to school every day, he had run up the hill for added defense. In my peripheral vision, noticing him readjusting his tie, I sensed his strength without turning to look.

Refocused toward the action, I could see from my vantage point that the young Hilltop Crips had taken a severe beating. Red blood was splattered upon their faces and clothing like paint unconsciously thrown against a vacant canvass.

As time began to take its normal pace, as if by magic, the sound of police sirens appeared like refereeing whistles in the wind.

Regaining eye contact with as many of the Bloods as possible, I yelled, "You're grown men. What is wrong with you?"

With the whistling of police sirens in the background, the woman hollering from her balcony, and Roman as backup, my confidence stabilized.

The Samoan quietly made the first move to break the stalemate. Releasing his mad dog stare down with me, he calmly closed the rear trunk lid of the red Cadillac, leisurely walked to the driver's side door, and got in. Without a spoken word, putting the car into gear, the rest of the goon squad jumped in. Never looking back, they sped away.

It was over.

As the police sirens diminished in the background, it occurred to me that we had been on our own the entire time. Gathering up the beaten young Crips, I waved and yelled a thank you to the lady in purple on the balcony.

The wanna-be Crips were bloody, shaken up, and silent.

Once in the security of the van, Roman and I passed out tissue from the toilet roll that was stashed under the driver's seat for emergency road trip bathroom stops. Little was said, I could see the fear in their eyes through the rearview mirror. Turning to my right from the driver seat and making eye contact, I calmly asked, "How about some hot fudge sundaes?"

The battered three appeared to be too stunned to respond. Their expressions were similar to old photos of World War I soldiers suffering from trench warfare shell shock. Calming down, having them as a captive audience in the van, I wanted to turn their "beat down" into a lesson.

As we were waiting in line at the drive-thru for our hot fudge sundaes, looking in the rearview mirror, I asked to no one in particular, "Do you really want to be a gangster?"

Pausing to let the question sink in and looking over at Roman, I nodded. Knowing the answer, but wanting the three young Crips to hear, I asked, "Roman, how many gangsters do we know of that are dead or in prison?"

The van was eerily quiet when Roman paused and responded, "I think at last count, we were up to over thirty-two that are dead or in prison." There was no response from the back seat and none was expected.

Moving forward after getting our hot fudge sundaes, I pulled into an empty parking space as Roman handed them their treats. "Do you really think that being a gang member is glamorous?" I asked.

Pausing to break open the small plastic bag of peanuts to place on top of my hot fudge sundae, I asked holding up another bag, "Nuts?"

Not receiving a response, after enjoying a taste I continued, "You got a sample of what it's like to be a banger. You're lucky they did not have guns."

Taking another enjoyable bite of warm melted chocolate over vanilla ice cream, I went on, "I have no idea what the Red guy was reaching for in the trunk, but I assure you that he was planning to beat your brains out with it!" I did not ask for a response and none was given. The five of us quietly ate our hot fudge sundaes, individually contemplating what could have happened.

Dropping the young Crips off one by one at their homes on the Hilltop, we took the opportunity to explain to whoever answered the door that they had been attacked for proclaiming to be Hilltop Crips. I got the feeling that their gang associations would be seriously readdressed.

Driving back to Region 5 Learning Center, glancing over at Roman, my expression said it all: "We were lucky today."

As I recall, I do not believe the young wanna-be Crips returned to Region 5. Not blaming them; after that beat down, I would have found another school too. My hope was that the experience changed their minds about gangs and that they went back to regular school to get a traditional education.

Red was emergency expelled for the remainder of the semester for instigating the young Crips getting "jumped and beat down."

What a bunch of punks; five on three is not what I would call a fair fight.

No other school would accept Red, so he was back with us for the start of the spring semester. As far as I was concerned, after instigating the gang fight, Red would never ride in the van with me again. But, as time passed and other potentially dangerous situations emerged, during the following semester, I forgave him.

Following the rules, Red begged and pleaded until I gave him one more chance in the platoon.

58. Knee Deep

n regard to Deanna's snow shoeing expedition, as we were taking the right-hand turn at the Eatonville turnoff by Alder Lake, I felt bad that Deanna and Angel were not able to go snowshoeing. I recall thinking that Boxcar Canyon might be enough excitement to satisfy their quest to prove that girls could do anything boys could do. Also, it was too early to return to school, and a visit to Boxcar Canyon would help to pass the time. "What problems could we run into there?" I confidently thought.

About a half mile from Eatonville, I took a right-hand turn onto a bouncy old gravel logging road. Just for added excitement, I accelerated slightly to get as much of a splash out of the huge milky brown mud puddles as safely possible.

After a half mile down the muddy logging road, we pulled over next to a pair of rusting train tracks. Snaking through the forest, the tracks led to a solitary black creosol-soaked wooden train trestle. Pausing to get the platoon's attention, I made it clear to everyone, "No one is to enter the river!" I sternly explained, "School district policies are quite specific—no water activities, at all!"

As we exited the van, I guided the platoon to a gouged-out section of the hillside. Pointing to the removed section of the dirt and gravel, I said, "This was someone's gold mining operation at one time." There was no interest, so I let the topic go.

Walking on the left-hand side of the rusting tracks, locating the overgrown trail, I took the platoon down a steep narrow muddy path to the river. I do not remember the name of the river, but the water was flowing very rapidly beneath the Boxcar Canyon train trestle. Unaware of the river's birth and until this day, I never gave it much thought. The raging river appeared to have sliced its way through a giant rock. Etched out by erosion over thousands of years, water cascades out of control under the wooden trestle. After quickly emerging, the fast flowing river calmly lays out into a wide gently rolling glossy stream.

Once down at the river's edge, several students began skipping rocks across the smooth surface of the water.

Interrupting the sounds of skimming rocks, Red pointed to a high point across the river to the cliffs. There was some graffiti writing and what seemed to be small jumping platforms from which to leap. "That's where we used to jump from," he proudly bragged.

I was proud of Red—he did not mention anything about being stoned when he said it.

Gathering up the platoon from the river, we meandered back up the steep dirt trail to the train tracks. Pointed I said, "The tracks are rusty. That's how you can tell that no trains have passed this way for some time."

Half way through my story, I was interrupted by several platoon members wanting to cross the train trestle which was about fifty feet above the river. Shifting my attention, I calmly denied their request.

Guarding the trestle entrance, I located a flat rock outcropping over the roaring river below. Sitting there hypnotized by the sound of the raging melted glacier water, I felt relaxed for the first time that day. Letting my guard down, several observant platoon members pointed to a trail along the erosion-etched side of the rock. I thought, "I've never noticed that before."

Deanna with a slight tilt of her head asked, "Can we see where the trail goes?"

Exploring the Boxcar Canyon area on several occasions, I had never found any danger to be aware of. "I guess it's safe—go ahead," I said as several other students returned to the river to throw rocks.

Being distracted, pointing down river, I yelled, "Hey, you rock throwers, down river there are two wrecked cars on the right-hand side barely visible!"

I could see everything from my seated vantage point and within my peripheral vision watched the platoon members hiking down-river to throw rocks at the submerged cars. Looking at the practically submerged rusting wrecks, the thought passed that they had probably been stolen from Tacoma and ditched here.

Posted high up on my rock pedestal, for a moment, I was relaxed and enjoying the peace and quiet. Then a weird feeling crept over me like a shadow. Besides the clanking of rocks bouncing off of rusting metal and splashing, it was too quiet. Something in the back of my mind put me on alert. I had a clear vantage point of the rock throwers when it hit me: "Where is the rest of the platoon?"

Standing up and listening for sounds, several seconds later, I heard Angel in a panic running down the tracks from the opposite direction of the narrow trail that disappeared around the rock face of Boxcar Canyon.

Trying to explain, I had to calm Angel down to understand her panicked ranting: "Deanna is stuck!"

From my left side three more platoon members were racing down the tracks toward us yelling something about Deanna, Red, and Avery being trapped on a cliff. Jarred quickly back into reality, noticing that their pants and shoes were muddy and soaking wet, I asked, "Where've you been?"

Their only response was, "You've got to come with us!"

After gathering the rock throwers, we followed the panicked hikers to a part of Boxcar Canyon that I was unfamiliar with. About a hundred yards from where I had been enjoying a rare few minutes of peace, a hidden trail that veered away from the train tracks and down into a gulch emerged. Once past the overgrown brush, the trail was well worn and used often. As we stumbled down the mud-soaked switchbacks of the trail, I was amazed that I had never been there before.

Glancing up from the well-worn path, I noticed that the river roared directly in front of us, slammed into the hillside, and raced around what appeared to be a giant rock face. From there, the river raged through the narrow Boxcar Canyon underneath the train trestle.

Once at the raging river's edge, I wondered, "Where are they?"

Listened before acting, to my left I could faintly hear sounds. Stumbling along the riverbank, following the voices, there they were.

Glancing up the side of a steep rock cliff, I saw three platoon members face-down against the rock wall. It appeared to me that the trail that they had followed from the Boxcar Canyon trestle had petered out and they were stranded fifteen to twenty feet above the roaring river.

As the momentary shock of the impending life-threatening situation passed, I asked a dumb question, "What are you guys doing?"

Red was the first to respond and yelled, "She is scared and will not move!"

Avery just looked at me saying nothing.

"Look, Avery, you and Red get down here now!" I demanded. After Red shadowed over Deanna, they climbed down and made it safely to the river's edge. Deanna was motionless.

"Okay, Deanna. It's your turn," I said in a calmer voice.

Turning her head slightly to face me, terror emanated from her eyes.

"Deanna, crab walk your way across the rock face. You will be okay," I said in a very calm and soothing voice.

Deanna just looked at me and shook her head. "I can't!"

Relaxed and breathing normally, my brain was kicking into gear. "Deanna, you will have to climb down or jump into the river!"

"I can't move!" she said in a trembling voice.

As time slowed down, I calmly instructed her, "I am going to get into the river and position myself so that I can quickly snatch you out when you jump!"

Sensing everyone staring at the back of my head, turning to look at the platoon, I told them, "Stay on this side of the river, and do not climb back up on that rock!" I was emphatic with my command. Silence followed as they looked upon me for strength.

Glancing around, Red was the first to speak up. "I'll jump in with her."

Surprised by Red's courage, it dawned on me that I was not a very good swimmer. Peering back at Deanna, a comical thought crossed my mind that she might end up having to save my life. I recall a frightening visualization of myself stumbling into the river trying to save Deanna and being swept away riding the rapids under the Boxcar Canyon train trestle to my death.

Pausing to think, my focus was caught off guard by the deafening sounds of the river crashing against the rock wall. Above the roar of the cascading river, I told Red; "There is no way that I am going to put you back on that—" Before I could finish my command, Avery, who was a Hilltop Crip, spoke up. "I'll go with him. I'm a good swimmer."

Without giving it much thought, impressed by the bravery that the two rival gang members were showing, we devised a plan.

After our huddle, I reinforced to both Avery and Red: "Climb back up on the rock cliff and help Deanna to turn facing toward the river."

I further coached, "Hold her hand, jump at the same time, and swim to the other side of the river." Making eye contact, I issued shared encouragement. "We can do this!"

As Avery and Red were climbing back up the rock face cliff to help petrified Deanna, crossing the knee-deep part of the river, I positioned myself at an angle to their jumping point. Estimating the rate of speed the river was traveling with the area that they would be jumping from, I positioned myself in the river accordingly. I calculated, if quick enough, I could grab the jumpers if they were unable to swim to the other side of the river.

Knowing something about rivers, I knew that the charging water that pounded off the rock face eroded an underwater trench, and that it was deeper than the depth of the river. I estimated, if we were lucky, that the water at the base of the cliff, at its deepest point, was hopefully six feet deep or more.

Standing knee-deep in freezing water as they prepared to jumped, I eased further into the quickly moving river. Seeing that Avery and Red had helped Deanna turn to face me, after a silent prayer, I yelled out over the roaring river, "Are you ready?"

Glancing up and focused my attention on the three of them; it was an amazing sight, a Hilltop Crip, a scared young lady, and an Eastside Blood. They were all hand-in-hand and ready to take the leap together. With time at a standstill, I thought, "Only at the Region 5."

Freezing my brains out, once more I asked, "Are you ready?"

As they shared a private conversation and nodded their heads, they jumped in unison, hand-in-hand.

As with most situations of this kind, time was running at a different pace. As they entered the water feet first, followed by three simultaneous splashes, I rushed to block their potential wash down the river.

Claiming to be a strong swimmer, Avery was true to his word and was the first to the opposite side of the riverbank.

Lucky for us, the river at their entry point was not as deep as I thought. Deanna and Red quickly scrambled to the shore as I veered toward them at an angle quickly corralling the three successful jumpers to the river's edge.

After a moment of silence, shaking from the icy cold water, the four of us just looked at each other, smiled, and shook our heads.

It was an awesome feeling—gang affiliations had dropped and prejudice was nonexistent. We stood in a circle of brotherhood and camaraderie.

Caught up in our successful rescue mission, smiling and shaking at the same time, we did not immediately notice being pelted by falling rain.

59. They All Talk

After crossing the river, scrambling up the slippery muddy trail, and changing into what dry clothes we had, everyone was safely tucked back into the school van like a nest of young eagles.

While eating lunch with the motor running and the heater on full blast, glancing in the rearview mirror, I could not have been more proud of the platoon. Then reality hit like the trembling of an emerging earthquake, I thought, "When word of this reaches Tacoma Schools, I am done."

Turning and blankly staring into the condensation-clouded windshield, barely hearing the rain pelting against the outer core of the van, a feeling of impending gloom swept over me. The feeling reminded me of a nightmare, a nightmare in which I was trying to run from unknown danger, but could not move.

Bringing me back from a distant part of my conscience, I faintly heard Deanna ask, "Darrell, what's wrong? We're safe."

Without turning to face her, the feeling of doom was overwhelming. In shell shock, I was contemplating the ramifications of having three students jump from a cliff into a raging river.

Deanna, who was very perceptive, asked again, "Darrell, what's wrong?"

"Deanna, I am done. This will be the last road trip that we ever take."

Sneaking a glance at Deanna through my peripheral vision, I could faintly see a puzzled expression on her face when she responded, "What do you mean? We are all safe."

Trying to glance out at Boxcar Canyon, my view was impeded by the droplets of condensation that had accumulated as a result of our perspiration. Pausing, trying to piece together the correct words, I confided in Deanna, "Once our principal finds out that the three of you jumped off a cliff into a raging river, I will be toast."

Expressing confidence, Deanna replied, "We can keep this a secret—no one will tell."

"Deanna, students always talk. No matter what the students say in this van, someone will tell. I have never known of an incident like this were a student did not blab to someone."

Deanna without responding to my comment turned and confronted the group. "Listen! If anyone finds out about us jumping into the river, Darrell will be fired." Deanna exaggerated to make her point. "We have to keep this a secret! You cannot tell anyone what happened here today!"

Red asked from the back seat, "What do you mean?"

Turning and facing the platoon members, my pride in their teamwork was immense. "You guys have done nothing wrong. I should never have brought you to Boxcar Canyon, and it's all my fault."

Pausing to maintain their attention, I said, "I just want you to know, when I am removed from Region 5 Learning Center, do not blame yourselves."

Letting my comments sink in, I followed up with, "The road trip program will be over. There will be no life sports, and I will be reassigned to another school." Exaggerating a little, I was following Deanna's lead.

Deanna added the final touch: "This is our secret!"

Turning forward, feeling the tension seeping out like the draining of a sieve, I felt at ease. Peering through an arc of dissipated condensation, the Boxcar Canyon trestle was clearly visible. Instinctively shifting the van into reverse, we slowly splashed our way out to the main road that led to Eatonville.

The following day, I expected Mack, the alternative education principal, to roar in rubbing his bald head in a panic. I was sure that after parents heard about the cliff-jumping incident; they would be on the phone immediately to Tacoma School District.

I would have.

As the days passed, my confidence in our promise to one another grew. They kept their promise.

Until the night I bumped into Deanna, I had only told two people the story—my youngest brother Roy and my cousin Rob. The cliff-jumping incident and the camaraderie that had emerged was another one of those rule-bending events that I will cherish for the rest of my life.

Looking into Deanna's deep brown eyes after so many years brought a warm feeling into my heart. I simple said, "You guys kept the secret."

Deanna, without breaking eye contact, softly expressed, "We all trusted you."

Acknowledgements:

Thisbook was written after my second presentation to the Tacoma School Board of Directors regarding the middle school's impact on the high school dropout rate that haunts Tacoma Schools. Directly after the school board meeting, my brother Roy Welch and I went out for dinner. Sensing frustration, Roy said, "You're an outsider, you have to be an insider to make change."

Pausing, he continued, "You should write your book and run for the school board." Roy's encouragement opened my perception to those possibilities.

My older sister, Cindy Hamlin was very helpful with her candid opinions and editing regarding the content of the manuscript. She will make a good author.

Indirectly, my sister Cathy Shively Hamlin provided encouragement through a conversation with my daughter Genevieve. One day Genevieve proclaimed to her, "Someday I want to be a writer." Cathy's response was simple, "Your dad has always been a writer."

I thank my mother Barbara Welch for her constant prayers.

In addition, I owe thanks to two childhood friends, Tim Shaffer and Fred Shenemen for their unrelenting friendship and faith in this project.

I thank my children Duncan and Genevieve Hamlin for listening to my rough draft nightly readings of the North Star Platoon. Their perceptions were extremely valuable.

I owe special thanks to my father and step mother, Richard and Lillian Hamlin. Without their continued editing and feed back this manuscript would not be what it is today.

I thank the students and dedicated staff of Region 5 Learning Center for giving me the educational opportunity to try new strategies with "at risk" students.

Lastly, I thank the Lord and my Guardian Angel for protecting and looking after us during our Life Sports excursions.

Thank you,

Darrell Hamlin